STEPPING

THROUGH

WINDOWS 3.1

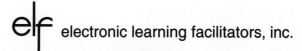 electronic learning facilitators, inc.

DRYDEN

Fort Worth   Philadelphia   San Diego   New York   Orlando   Austin   San Antonio
Toronto   Montreal   London   Sydney   Tokyo

Editor in Chief: Robert A. Pawlik
Acquisitions Editor: Emily Thompson
Assistant Project Editor: Cathy Spitzenberger
Production Manager: Trisha Dianne
Book Designer: Priscilla Mingus

ISBN: 0-03-096901-8
Library of Congress Catalog Card Number: 92-72957
Printed in the United States of America

2 3 4 5 6 7 8 9 0 1   054   9 8 7 6 5 4 3 2 1

The Dryden Press
Harcourt Brace Jovanovich

PREFACE

Stepping Through Windows 3.1 is a comprehensive workbook and reference guide designed to prepare you to work with Microsoft Windows^{TM} 3.1 on an IBM or IBM-compatible PC. This book is intended for students who are familiar with DOS, especially DOS version 5.0.

If you're not familiar with the PC or with DOS, read Appendix A first. This appendix provides details about PC hardware and software.

This workbook is divided into 10 chapters. Each chapter includes a discussion of new concepts, several activities where those concepts are practiced, and "On Your Own" sessions that let you experiment with what you have learned.

When you finish this course, you should be able to:

- start Windows

- identify the parts of the Windows screen

- run Windows and DOS applications under Windows

- use the Windows accessories

- customize your Windows environment

- use the File Manager to organize files and directories on your PC

- use the Control Panel to control and customize your Windows environment

- install printers and fonts

- add, delete, or change icons in the Program Manager

- create and edit Program Information Files (PIF)

- understand Object Linking and Embedding (OLE)

Organization

Stepping Through Windows 3.1 has the following components:

- Chapter overview and objectives

- Instructional notes for each topic

- Step-by-step references to accomplish each function

- Illustrations and screen facsimiles

- Guided hands-on activities

- Unguided "On Your Own" exercises

- Quick Checks at the end of each chapter

- Appendices

- Index

Guide to the Workbook

Although *Stepping Through Windows 3.1* is comprehensive, it is *not* a user's manual. Refer to the *Microsoft Windows User's Guide* for information not contained in this workbook.

The best way to use this book is sequentially — step-by-step — since many of the activities build on concepts developed and files created in previous units.

Similarly, most activities and exercises build on each other. If you follow the steps to complete one exercise, you should be able to begin the next exercise without additional preparation.

Do not close, exit, or minimize a program unless you are instructed to do so.

Conventions

You'll see the following conventions in this book:

- Nonalphabetic keys to be pressed are enclosed in brackets. Examples: [F1], [PgDn], [Enter].

- Keys used in combination with the [Ctrl], [Alt], or [Shift] keys are shown in this manner: [Ctrl][F2]. The [Ctrl] key is held down while the [F2] key is pressed and released.

- Hands-on activities have numbered steps to distinguish them from reference material.

- Most activities have an On Your Own task to reinforce your knowledge. If you are unable to complete the task, ask your instructor for assistance.

- Quick Checks and On Your Own activities are indicated by the checkmark symbol shown to the left.

- Notes for your attention are indicated by the note paper symbol shown to the left.

- Important cautionary information is indicated by the exclamation point symbol shown to the left.

- Items of importance or procedures are marked with bullets as in this conventions list.

- Text shown in italics like the following is either text to be typed or an action to be performed by the student:

    type **Acme Letter** and press [Enter]

Student Disk

The student disk that accompanies this book contains the following directories and files:

A:\	text.wri	A:\MEMOS\SMITH
acme.bmp	todolist.txt	other.mem
acme.wri	training.wri	train.mem
address.crd	travel.mem	
art.bmp		A:\WAKEUP
artmemo.wri	A:\FRAGCHEK	readme
benefits.let	frageval.bat	wakeup.exe
benfinal.let	fragtext.mem	wakeup.num
busy.cal		wakeup.txt
chapter1.let	A:\MEMOS	
logo.bmp	A:\MEMOS\JONES	
printers.mem	printers.mem	
	travel.mem	

Blank Diskette

A blank (preferably unformatted) double-sided, double-density diskette is required for Activity 5.5.

System Setup

The activities presented here assume a system configuration for each workstation as follows:

- An IBM or IBM-compatible computer with a minimum of 2MB RAM.

- DOS version 5.0.

- A bootable hard disk designated as drive C.

- A floppy disk drive designated as drive A: in which the student disk will be inserted. If another floppy disk drive is to be used for the student disk, that drive designator should be substituted in any activity that refers to drive A:.

- Windows 3.1 software installed on drive C: in the directory C:\WINDOWS. If another drive or directory is used, that should be substituted in any activity that refers to C:\WINDOWS. If Windows 3.1 needs to be installed, refer to Appendix B.

- Access by each workstation to a printer.

- A mouse input device. Keyboard equivalents for most mouse procedures are available, but a mouse is assumed to be the primary input device for all activities.

Acknowledgments

We would like to acknowledge the following individuals for making *Stepping Through Windows 3.1* possible: Lucille Parker, Karen Penn, and Ken Robertson who developed and wrote the book; Carol Derenak who reviewed and tested the activities; Karen Penn and Lisa White who produced it; and Carolyn Adler who conceived, planned, and produced it.

We welcome all questions and comments from users of this workbook.

electronic learning facilitators, inc.
7910 Woodmont Avenue
Bethesda, Maryland 20814

Contents

Preface		**iii**
Chapter 1	**A First Look into Windows**	**1**
	Windows Features	2
	What Does Windows Include?	2
	What Does Windows Look Like?	6
	Getting Started	7
	Program Manager	8
	Parts of a Window	9
	Using the Mouse	10
	Maximizing and Minimizing	12
	Opening Program Groups	13
	Closing a Group Window	15
	Using Windows Help	16
	Starting Help	17
	Using Scroll Bars	18
	Quitting Windows	21
	Quick Check	*22*
Chapter 2	**Windows Basics**	**23**
	The Clock Program	24
	Starting a Program	24
	Sizing and Moving a Window	25
	Minimizing vs. Closing	27
	Quitting a Program	27
	Using the Calculator	28
	Entering Calculations	29
	The Calendar Program	33
	Using Pull-Down Menus	34
	Opening Files	35

Moving to a Specific Date 39
Entering Text 40
Saving Your New Calendar 42
Quick Check 43

Chapter 3   **More Desktop Accessories**   **45**

Entering Text in the Notepad 46
Cursor and Pointer 47
Entering and Editing Text 47
Selecting Text 48
Cut, Copy, and Paste 50
The Cardfile 52
Transferring Text 55
Switching Between Applications 56
The Task List 56
Switching Between Programs 58
Quick Check 59

Chapter 4   **Other Accessories and Techniques**   **61**

Using Write as a Word Processor 62
Formatting 64
Fonts 66
Character Map 67
Using Paintbrush to Create Graphics 69
Drawing Basics 72
Adding Text 76
Pasting a Graphic 77
The Recorder 78
Quick Check 85

Chapter 5   **The File Manager**   **87**

The File Manager 87
Managing Files and Directories 92
Deleting Files 93
Working with Files 95
Quick Check 98

Chapter 6	**The Control Panel**	**99**

The Control Panel 99
Changing Colors 103
The Windows Desktop 105
Windows Initialization Files 108
   INI File Format 109
   The WIN.INI File 110
   The SYSTEM.INI File 111
Using Sysedit 112
   Quick Check *114*

Chapter 7	**Fonts and Printing**	**115**

About Fonts 116
Screen Fonts 117
   Raster Fonts 117
   Vector Fonts 117
   Outline Fonts (TrueType) 117
Printer Fonts 118
   Device Fonts 118
   Software Fonts 118
Selecting a Printer 119
   Configuring a Printer 120
   Setting Up a Printer 122
Printing from Windows 123
   The Print Manager 123
   When Problems Occur 125
   Print Manager Options 125
Drag and Drop Printing 126
Printing from Non-Windows
   Applications 127
   Quick Check *128*

Chapter 8	**Program Manager**	**129**

About Program Manager 129
   Program Groups and Items 130
   Arranging Windows and Icons 130
   The Options Menu 132

Creating Program Groups   134
  Adding Items to a Group   136
  Adding Documents to a Group   136
  Another Way to Add Items   138
Deleting Items and Groups   138
Using the StartUp Group   140
  Quick Check   *142*

Chapter 9   **Working with DOS Applications   143**

Non-Windows Applications
  Under Windows   144
Starting a DOS Program   144
Manipulating DOS Applications   146
Setting up Popular DOS Applications   147
Program Information Files   148
Preparing to Use the PIF   150
Cutting and Pasting between
  DOS Applications   152
  Copying to a DOS Application   152
  Copying from a DOS Application   154
  Quick Check   *157*

Chapter 10   **Sharing Information Between
                  Applications   159**

What Is OLE?   160
  Servers and Clients   160
  Linking or Embedding   161
  Embedding an Object   162
  Linking an Object   167
Object Packages   169
Using the Object Packager   171
  Quick Check   *175*

Appendix A	**The Computer System**	**177**
	Computer Hardware	178
	Input Devices	180
	Output Devices	182
	Dual I/O Devices	185
	Network Resources	187
	Computer Software	187
	Applications	189
	Operating Systems	194

Appendix B	**Installation and Setup**	**195**
	Hardware Configurations	195
	Installing with Setup	197
	Installing Applications	201
	Using Setup for Maintenance	202
	Changing Device Drivers	203
	Setup Problems	204

Appendix C	**Optimizing Windows**	**205**
	Memory Overview	205
	Effective Memory Usage	208
	What Does Windows Require?	212
	Operating Modes	213
	Managing Your Hard Drive	215
	Swap Files	216
	Disk Caching	220

Appendix D	**Windows and Networks**	**223**
	About Networks	223
	Supported Networks	224
	Network Installations	224
	Connecting Network Drives	228
	Printing	229
	Optimizing	229

Appendix E | **Troubleshooting**   **231**

Problem-Solving Procedure   231
Setup Problems   233
DOS Mode Failure   233
Operational Problems   235
Standard Mode   235
386 Enhanced Mode   237

Index   **239**

Chapter
1

A First Look into Windows

Windows™ is a graphical operating environment that provides a different way to interact with your IBM-type computer. Windows is an environment, not an operating system. This means that your computer must have DOS to run Windows.

There is a key difference between Windows and DOS and between applications that were written for them. When you work with DOS, you type commands at a prompt. You must know the commands as well as the correct syntax to make them work. Instead of the DOS prompt, Windows provides you with a graphical interface of menus and icons. With Windows, you interact with pictures and menus using a mouse rather than the keyboard as the primary input device.

When you first begin to work in a new environment, you need to learn new concepts, terminology, and techniques. This chapter introduces Windows 3.1 features and capabilities and presents information you need to start working with Windows.

- Start the Windows program

- Identify the parts of a window

- Use the mouse to select and drag

- Maximize and minimize a window

- Open and close a program group

- Use Windows Help

- Use scroll bars

- Exit Windows

Windows Features

Windows is a working environment for your computer that allows you to work with several programs at once and to do so through a consistent, graphical interface. With Windows, you work with items on your computer screen much the way you'd work with them on your desk—opening files, moving things around, temporarily putting one task aside to work with another, and so on. Here are some of the things that Windows 3.1 can do for you.

- Windows has a *graphical user interface (GUI)* that allows you to perform tasks by selecting from menus and recognizable screen objects called icons.

- Windows programs share a *common look and feel* so that learning a new program takes less time. Whether you're using a spreadsheet, a word processor, or another application, you always do certain tasks — like opening a file and printing — the same way.

- Windows provides *multitasking* capability that lets you work with more than one application at a time and quickly switch from one to the other. You can, for example, have both your spreadsheet and word processor programs available at the same time and move easily between them.

- Windows lets you easily *transfer and share information* from one Windows program to another.

Produced by Microsoft®, the Windows product has been in development since 1985, when Windows 1.0 was copyrighted. The current version of the product, Windows 3.1, was released in April of 1992.

What Does Windows Include?

The heart of Windows is the Program Manager. Inside the Program Manager, basic Windows 3.1 initially contains five program groups: Accessories, Main, StartUp, Applications, and Games.

Accessories In the Accessories group you'll find a useful group of desktop applications. Most of the applications in the Accessories group are shown in Table 1-1. The table describes the application and shows where in this book it is discussed.

Table 1-1 Accessories Group

Application	Purpose	Where Described
Clock	Clock	Chapter 2
Calculator	Desktop calculator with standard and scientific modes	Chapter 2
Calendar	Calendar for scheduling appointments and setting alarms	Chapter 2
Notepad	Editor for creating and editing text files	Chapter 3
Cardfile	Electronic card file for creating and indexing data in card format	Chapter 3
Write	Word processing	Chapter 4
Character Map	Displays characters and allows them to be selected and copied	Chapter 4
Paintbrush	Creating and editing graphics	Chapter 4
Recorder	Recorder of keystrokes for playback in Windows and Windows applications	Chapter 4
Object Packager	Packages objects for linking and embedding in Windows applications	Chapter 10

The Accessories group also includes several applications that require special hardware to be used. These applications are shown below and are not otherwise covered in this book.

Table 1-2 Additional Accessories

Application	Purpose
Terminal	Communications with remote computers
Media Player	Controls a media player like a videodisk or video tape player
Sound Recorder	Records sound and stores it digitally

Main The Main group's purpose is to provide support to the Windows environment. It contains utility programs that let you work with the features of Windows that support the other programs. Applications in the Main group are shown in Table 1-3.

Table 1-3 Main Group

Application	Purpose	Where Described
File Manager	Manipulate and manage files, directories, and disks; start applications	Chapter 5
Control Panel	Controls the Windows environment including screen colors, fonts, printers, etc.	Chapter 6
Print Manager	Receives and handles print requests from Windows applications	Chapter 7
PIF Editor	Editor for creating and editing Program Information Files for DOS applications	Chapter 9
MS-DOS Prompt	Method for temporarily accessing DOS	Chapter 9
Clipboard Viewer	Method for viewing and saving the contents of the Windows Clipboard	Refer to your Microsoft Windows User's Guide
Windows Setup	Program for changing setup options and setting up applications	Appendix B

Other Program Groups You may or may not have an Applications group. This group includes any applications added during the Windows setup process (see Appendix B). If you have not installed any programs other than Windows on your computer's hard disk, there may be no Applications group.

The Games group contains two games — Solitaire and Minesweeper. As you become more familiar with Windows, you will probably enjoy teaching yourself to use these games.

Finally, there is the StartUp group, which will be empty when you first use Windows (see Chapter 9 for more information on using this group).

What Does Windows Look Like?

Unless you've modified the default setup, Program Manager is the first window you see when you start Windows. Program Manager may be in a rectangular window that fits on the screen or fills the entire screen. Alternatively, it may be an icon at the bottom of the screen.

Inside Program Manager, you'll see program groups. These groups may appear as icons or as windows inside the Program Manager. In most cases there'll be five groups — Accessories, Games, Main, StartUp, and Applications. But if you did not choose to install applications during the Windows setup process, there will be no Applications group, or there may be other groups created by another user.

Once you start working with applications, Windows may have many looks depending on what you're doing — whether you want to work with several applications, or are concentrating on just one. Your computer screen may have a single window like the Program Manager open, or it may resemble a busy desktop with a calendar, clock, and notepad all visible at once.

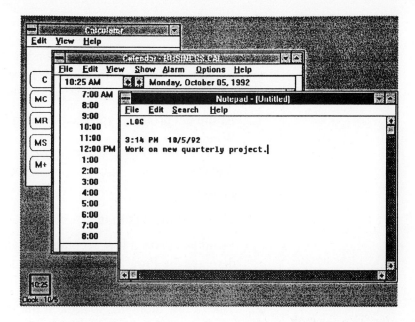

On the desktop above, the Notepad is in use. It's on top of the other programs ready for you to enter text. You may quickly switch to any of the other programs as your needs change.

Getting Started

If Windows has been correctly installed on your computer, you can start it from the DOS C:\ prompt by typing **win** and pressing **[Enter]**.

After it starts, Windows takes a few seconds to load and then displays the Program Manager window with several program group icons. What you see when Windows loads depends on whether Windows has been previously run on the computer and on how it was exited. A typical opening screen is described in the remainder of this section.

Activity 1.1	Starting Windows

Starting Windows

After Windows has been installed on your computer, you're ready to proceed. In this activity you'll start the Windows program.

1. At the C:\ prompt, type the command to start Windows.

   type **win**

   press [Enter]

   That's all there is to it.

   Windows takes a few seconds to load and then displays the Program Manager window with several program group icons.

2. Take a few moments to look at the Program Manager window. It should resemble the figure below.

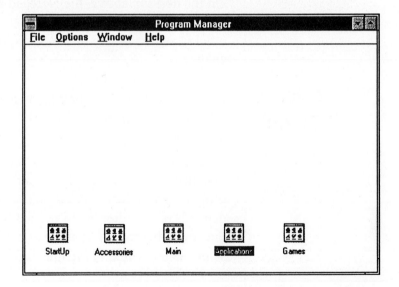

Program Manager

The Program Manager is a special Window. It is the foundation on which all the rest of Windows stands; it manages the other programs. When you start Windows you're starting the Program Manager. When you close or exit the Program Manager you're exiting Windows.

In the next few pages, you'll use the Program Manager window to learn a few of the terms which apply to all Windows programs.

Parts of a Window

The parts of a typical window are shown and described below. Some of the terms may be new to you now, but they will become familiar as you go along.

Take a few minutes now to learn the names for the various parts of a window. You'll need to know them for the following activities.

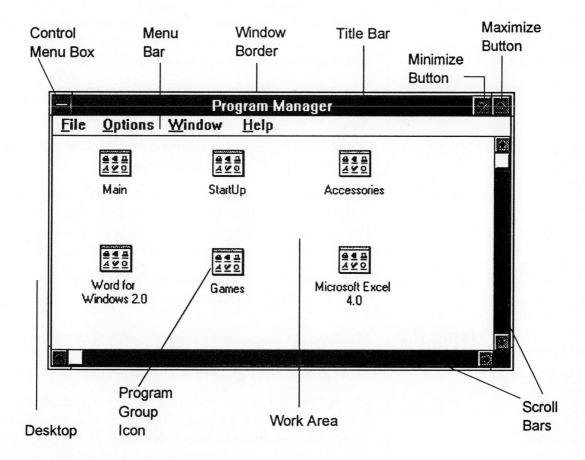

Window Borders	Each window has a border to define its perimeter.
Title Bar	The name of the window is in the title bar directly below the top border.
Control-Menu Box	On the left end of the title bar is the Control-menu box. When selected, this box provides a menu for sizing, moving, or closing the window.
Sizing Buttons	The two arrow buttons on the right end of the title bar may be used to size a window. The down arrow is called the *minimize* button and is used to shrink a window to an icon. The up arrow is called the *maximize* button and is used to enlarge a window to fill the screen. If a window already fills the screen, the maximize button will be replaced by a two-headed arrow called the *restore* button. The restore button returns a window to its intermediate size.
Menu Bar	The menu bar provides a selection of command menus.
Work Area	The work area is the space inside the window.
Program Group Icon	An icon is a small picture representing a window. The icon provides access to a group of programs.
Scroll Bars	When a window contains more information than is currently visible inside the window borders, scroll bars will appear at the right or bottom edge of the window. A window may have horizontal or vertical scroll bars or both.
Desktop	The desktop is the area outside the Program Manager when its window is not maximized.

Using the Mouse

Windows is designed to be used primarily with a mouse, but can also be used with a keyboard. Throughout this book, preference is given to mouse methods.

Perhaps the easiest way to control the mouse is to place your hand lightly on the base of the mouse with your wrist resting on your desk and your index finger lying lightly on the left mouse button. As you move the mouse on your desk, the mouse pointer moves on the screen.

- You *select* an item by moving the pointer onto the item, then pressing and releasing the left mouse button. This is called **clicking.**

- You *move* an object by moving the pointer onto the object, pressing and holding down the left mouse button, and moving the pointer to the desired location. You release the button at the desired location. This is called **dragging**.

- You *open* a program group or program by moving the pointer onto the item and clicking the left mouse button two times quickly: click-click. This is called **double-clicking**.

In the next two activities you'll practice using the mouse in the Program Manager window to select and drag.

| Activity 1.2 | ## Selecting with the Mouse |

1. Select the Control-menu box.

click Control-menu box

2. Select a program group.

click the Accessories icon

The Control menu for the Accessories group appears.

3. Select the Help menu and then close it.

click Help

click elsewhere in the work area

The menu disappears.

| Activity 1.3 | ## Dragging with the Mouse |

1. Move a program group icon.

drag the Accessories group icon to the right or left

2. Try to move icons beyond the window border.

drag the leftmost group farther to the left

drag a group icon toward the bottom border.

What happened? You cannot drag an icon outside the window border. You may still be able to see part of the icons you moved. Also, horizontal and vertical scroll bars appear to allow you to scroll the window.

On Your Own

1. Drag the icons back to their former position or click the scroll arrows to make all icons visible again.

2. Experiment with dragging icons and with clicking the scroll arrows.

Maximizing and Minimizing

Examine the Program Manager title bar. At the right end of the title bar are the maximize and minimize buttons. You can change the size of the window in several ways.

- Clicking the maximize button enlarges the Program Manager window to fill the entire screen. The maximize button is then replaced by a restore button.

- Clicking the restore button returns Program Manager to its previous size.

- Clicking the minimize button shrinks the window to an icon.

Once a window has been minimized to an icon, you double-click the icon to restore the window to the screen.

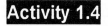

Maximizing and Minimizing

1. Maximize the Program Manager window.

click the maximize button

The window should now fill the screen.

2. Restore the window to its previous size.

click the restore button

The window is returned to its previous size.

3. Minimize the window.

click the minimize button

The window shrinks to an icon on the desktop.

4. Restore the window from the icon.

double-click the icon

The window returns to its previous size.

Note: You can also maximize a window by double-clicking in its title bar. If a window is maximized, double-clicking in the title bar restores it.

Opening Program Groups

In order to access the programs that are part of a program group, you must open the group. You open a program group by double-clicking its icon. When you do so, the group window will open inside the Program Manager window. If, for example, you double-click the Accessories icon, the Accessories group window opens, as shown in the figure below.

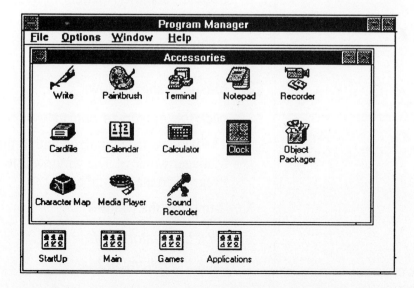

Notice that a program group window has many of the same parts as the Program Manager window, including a title bar, Control-menu box, and minimize and maximize buttons. Program group windows, however, do *not* have menu bars.

You can maximize a program group window by clicking the window's maximize button. Note the following about maximizing program group windows:

- Maximizing a program group window will only enlarge the group window to fill the Program Manager window, not to fill the entire screen.

- When you maximize a program group window, the title of the group will appear in the Program Manager title bar.

Once you've maximized a program group window, you can minimize it by first clicking the restore button and then clicking the program group window's minimize button.

Activity 1.5 Opening a Program Group

1. Open a program group.

   double-click the Accessories icon

   Examine the Accessories group window for a moment. Notice the window title bar, Control-menu box, and sizing buttons.

2. Maximize the window.

   click the maximize button

   The window is maximized within the Program Manager window. The window title is shown in the Program Manager title bar.

3. Minimize the window.

   click the restore button

   click the minimize button

The group window appears as an icon within the Program Manager window.

On Your Own

1. Use the mouse to open the Main program group.

2. Practice maximizing, restoring, and minimizing.

Closing a Group Window

Most windows have a Control menu. The Control menu can be used to maximize, restore, or minimize a window, but it's most often used to close a window.

- You select the Control menu for a window by clicking the Control-menu box.

- You select the Control menu for an icon by clicking the icon. The Control menu contains a list of commands, as shown here.

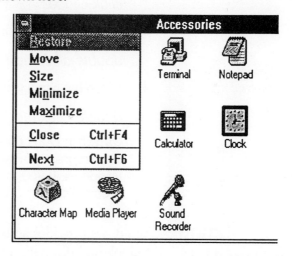

- You can select a command from the Control menu by clicking the command.

- The command to close a window is Close.

- An even faster way to close a window is to double-click the Control-menu box.

Note: When you close an application window (i.e., a window with a menu bar), you're quitting the application. This means that if you double-click the Program Manager Control-menu box, you'll be exiting Windows.

Activity 1.6

Using the Control Menu

1. Open the Accessories program group with the Control menu.

   click the Accessories icon

   click Restore

2. Close the Accessories group with the Control menu.

   click the Control-menu box

   click Close

3. Open the Main program group.

   double-click the Main icon

4. Close the Main group quickly.

   double-click the Control-menu box

   Caution: Don't double-click the Control-menu box in the Program Manager title bar unless you want to exit Windows. If you make a mistake, click Cancel or press [Esc].

Using Windows Help

Windows provides an on-line Help facility that allows you to look up information about functions and features while you work. You can use Help to answer questions about a task you want to perform or a command you're about to use.

Help is available in Windows whenever you see a Help menu choice. All of the applications that are supplied with Windows (except the Clock) include Help. Other Windows applications usually include Help as well. Check the application's documentation for more information.

Starting Help

You can start Help by clicking Help on the menu bar, then selecting Contents from the menu or by pressing [F1] on your keyboard. When you do so, a Help window opens. The Help Contents window for the Program Manager is shown below.

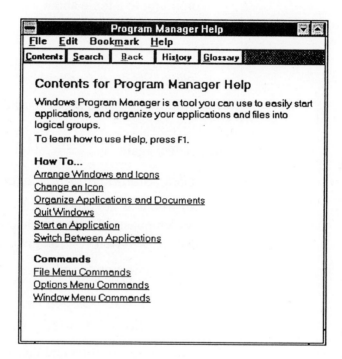

Once you've started Help, you can browse through information, search for specific topics, or look up terms in a glossary. You'll practice some of these techniques in the next activity.

Activity 1.7

Using Help

1. Start Help.

click Help

select Contents

2.   Observe the mouse pointer.

move the mouse pointer over the underlined topics

The mouse pointer turns into a hand when you're pointing to a topic about which there is additional information.

3.   Select a topic.

click "Start an Application"

Additional topics about starting an application are displayed.

4.   Select again.

click "Starting an Application from a Group"

Instructions are presented. Notice that several terms are emphasized with a dashed underline. These are terms for which you can get a definition.

5.   Get a definition for a term.

click the word "group"

A definition of the word pops up.

6.   Close the definition and the Help window.

click anywhere in the Help window

double-click the Help window Control-menu box

Using Scroll Bars

Sometimes when you're working with Help, there will be more information available than fits in the Help window. In Help (and throughout Windows) when this is the case, scroll bars will appear so that you can scroll the information within the window.

There is an arrow button at the top of the scroll bar, the Up scroll arrow. The arrow button at the bottom of the scroll bar is the Down scroll arrow. Somewhere in between the two is the scroll box. You can scroll as follows:

• Each click on an arrow moves the window or list by one line. Holding down the mouse button will scroll through the window or list.

• Clicking in the scroll bar above or below the scroll box moves the window or list by one page.

• Dragging the scroll box moves your position in the window or list proportionally to the distance the box has been moved.

• Dragging the box to the top or bottom of the scroll bar moves you to the beginning or end of the window or list.

You may have either a horizontal or vertical scroll bar, or sometimes both. Horizontal scroll bars are for moving sideways, vertical are for moving up and down.

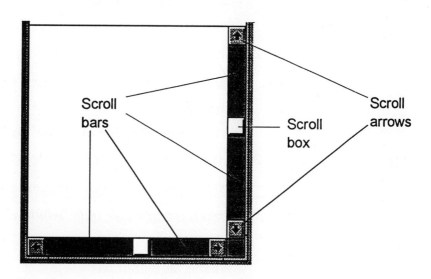

In the next activity, you'll get some practice with scroll bars while using the Windows Help glossary.

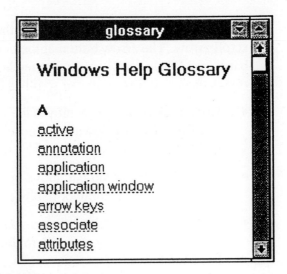

Activity 1.8 | **Scrolling in Help**

1. Start Help and examine the glossary.

   select Help, Contents
   click the Glossary button
   The glossary window opens on top of the Help window.

2. Look up a term in the glossary.

   click the down scroll arrow until "close" is visible
   click "close"
   What is the definition of "close" in Help?

3. After removing the definition, look up another term.

   click elsewhere in the Glossary window
   drag the scroll box until "window" is visible
   click "window"
   What is the definition?

4. Close the definition, the Glossary, and the Help window.

   click elsewhere

double-click the Glossary window Control-menu box

double-click the Help window Control-menu box

On Your Own

1. Try the procedure again.

2. Look up other terms in the Glossary and use the scroll bars to move around.

3. Close the Glossary and the Help window when you finish.

Quitting Windows

When you're ready to stop working with Windows, you can exit easily by using the Program Manager's Control menu:

• Click the Control-menu box and then click Close.

OR

• Double-click the Control-menu box.

Either way, you'll be asked to confirm the exit. To do so, click OK.

Activity 1.9

Exiting Windows

1. Exit Windows and return to the DOS prompt.

double-click the Program Manager Control-menu box

2. Confirm your decision to exit.

click OK

Quick Check

See if you can answer the following questions. Use Windows to verify your answers.

1. How do you start Windows 3.1?

2. Name the various parts of the window in the figure below.

3. How can you maximize a window? Minimize? Restore?

4. How do you open a program group?

5. How do you close a window?

6. List two ways to start Help.

7. How do you exit Windows?

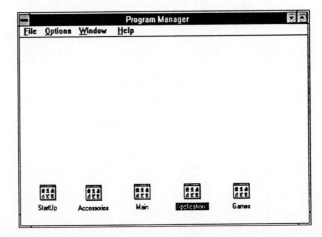

Chapter
2

Windows Basics

Overview

Now that you've learned some Windows concepts and terminology, you're ready to explore some more Windows techniques. Along the way, you'll continue to use what you've learned and to add useful new information as well.

This chapter introduces some of the programs from the Accessories group that are referred to as *desktop accessories*. These programs are called "desktop" accessories because they replicate on your computer screen items that you might have on your desk — a clock, a calculator, or a calendar, for example.

While you're learning about the Windows Clock, Calculator, and Calendar accessories in this chapter, you'll really be practicing techniques that apply to other Windows programs.

Objectives

- Start and stop a program
- Use the Clock program
- Move and size a window
- Use the Calculator program
- Use the Calendar program to schedule appointments
- Use pull-down menus
- Use dialog boxes
- Open and save files

The Clock Program

Among the Windows accessories, the Clock is probably the simplest to use. The clock displays the time and, optionally, the date.

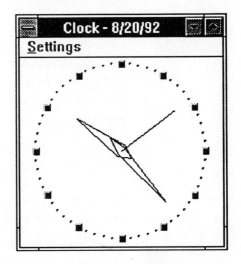

Using the Clock program, you'll learn how to start a program, move and size a window, and quit a program.

Starting a Program

Each icon within a program group represents a program. You start a program by double-clicking its icon. When you've started a program, it runs in its own window on the screen.

- You can use the maximize and minimize buttons to change the size of a program window.

- When you minimize a program window, the program continues to run and usually appears as an icon on the desktop.

- You can restore the program window by double-clicking the icon.

You'll practice this in the next activity.

Activity 2.1

Starting the Clock

Before beginning this activity, make sure the Program Manager window is open on the screen and not maximized. If the Accessories group is not open, open it now.

1. Locate the Clock icon in the Accessories group.

    double-click the Clock icon

    The Clock program window opens on the screen. If you're starting the Clock program for the first time, a standard analog clock is displayed.

2. Maximize the Clock window.

    click the maximize button in the Clock window

    The Clock window fills the entire screen and hides the Program Manager.

3. Minimize the Clock window.

    click the minimize button

    Notice that the Clock icon appears outside the Program Manager window on the desktop. The Clock program continues to run as an icon.

4. Restore the Clock.

    double-click the Clock icon on the desktop

5. Now return the Clock window to its intermediate size.

    click the restore button

    Leave the Clock on screen for the next activity.

Sizing and Moving a Window

You already know how to change the size of a window using the maximize and minimize buttons. Now you'll see how to resize the proportions of a window by dragging its borders.

When you move the mouse pointer over a window border, the pointer changes to a double-headed arrow. At the corners of a window, the mouse pointer changes to a diagonal double-headed arrow.

- Dragging the top or bottom border sizes the window vertically.

- Dragging either side border sizes the window horizontally.

- Dragging a window corner sizes the whole window proportionally.

You can move a window by dragging its title bar to a new location. You cannot, however, move a window that is maximized.

Activity 2.2 | Sizing and Moving the Clock Window

The Clock window must be open on your screen and not maximized.

1. Adjust the mouse pointer until it becomes a two-headed arrow.

   move the pointer over the top border of the Clock window

2. Resize the window vertically.

   drag the top or bottom border

3. Resize the window horizontally so that it takes up half the screen.

   move the pointer over a side border

   drag the border to the middle of the screen

4. Move the Clock window to the right.

   position the mouse pointer in the title bar

   drag the Clock to the right

   Notice that an image of the window border moves as you move the mouse. When you release the mouse button, the window moves to the new position.

Minimizing vs. Closing

When you are just opening and closing program groups, you achieve the same result whether you minimize a program group window or close it. In both cases, the program group window becomes an icon in the Program Manager window. But when you're running a program, minimizing and closing are *significantly different* operations with different effects.

- When you **minimize** a program, the program continues to run as an icon on your desktop, and you can return to the program by restoring the icon to a window.

- When you **close** a program window, the program stops operating.

If you want to keep the Clock available on your screen while you work with other accessories, you can minimize the Clock. When you no longer need the Clock, you can quit the program by closing its window.

Quitting a Program

To **quit** a program, you close the program window. You can close a window with the Control-menu box in two ways:

- Click the Control-menu box, then select Close

  OR

- Double-click the Control-menu box.

The Clock window should be open on your screen. In the next activity, you'll minimize, then close the window to exit the program.

Activity 2.3

Closing the Clock Window

1. Minimize the Clock window.

click the minimize button

Notice that the Clock icon appears on the desktop, and the program continues to run.

2. Restore the Clock.

double-click the Clock icon on the desktop

3. Quit the Clock program.

   double-click the Clock Control-menu box

   The Clock window closes.

On Your Own

You've decided to keep a minimized Clock on your desktop, but you'd prefer digital settings, as shown below.

1. Start the Clock.

2. Change the Clock settings to digital. (HINT: Click Settings, then click Digital)

3. Practice sizing and moving the Clock window.

4. Minimize the Clock.

Using the Calculator

The Windows Calculator lets you perform routine calculations without leaving your computer to search for a desktop calculator. You can start the Calculator quickly any time you need it. If you'll be using it extensively, you can leave it running as an icon on your desktop.

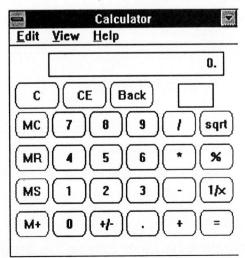

The Calculator provides two modes of operation: standard and scientific. In this section, you'll work with the Calculator in standard mode. While using the Calculator, you'll also practice searching in Help and learn a simple method for switching between open windows.

Activity 2.4

Starting the Calculator

The Program Manager window should be open and not maximized. If the Accessories group is not open, open it now.

1. Start the Calculator program.

double-click the Calculator icon in the Accessories group

The Calculator program opens in its own window on the screen. Notice that the Calculator does not have a maximize button.

2. Make the Calculator an icon.

click the minimize button

The Calculator appears as an icon on the desktop.

3. Restore the Calculator.

double-click the Calculator icon

4. Move the Calculator.

drag the title bar to a new location

Note: The Calculator is a fixed-size window. You cannot maximize it; nor can you size it by dragging its border.

Entering Calculations

Entering arithmetic calculations is straightforward: you enter the number, choose an operator (+, −, *, /), enter additional numbers and operators, then click the equals sign (=) to see the result.

If you make a mistake while entering a number, you can click the Back button to remove digits, or you can click the CE button to delete the entire number. When you're finished with a result, you can click the C button to clear the display.

Activity 2.5	## Entering Calculations

The Calculator should be open on your screen.

1.   Add two numbers, 123 and 456.

click 123

click the + (plus) button

click 456

click the = button

What is the result?

2.   Clear the display.

click the C button

3.   Multiply two numbers, 56 and 89.

click 56

*click the * button*

click 89

click the = button

What is the result?

Activity 2.6	## Searching for Help

1.   For more information about the Calculator, try searching in Help.

click Help

click Search for Help on...

scroll through the list

select Memory, Using

click Show Topics

click Go To

2. Read the Help information and get more details.

   scroll the Help window until the information about the memory buttons appears

   click the Contents button

   select Use Memory Functions

3. Close the Help window.

   double-click the Control-menu box in the Calculator window

In the next activity, you'll practice what you just learned about using the Calculator's memory functions.

Activity 2.7 | ## Using the Memory Functions

The Calculator should be open on your screen.

1. Clear the display and add two numbers, 67 and 879.

   click the C button

   click 67

   click the + button

   click 879

   click the = button

   What is the result?

2. Store the result in memory and clear the display.

   click the MS button

   click the C button

   The MS button stores the displayed number in memory.

3. Add two more numbers, 75 and 97; then add the total to the number in memory.

   click 75

   click the + button

click 97

click the = button

click the M+ button

4. Display the value in memory.

click the MR button

What is the result?

Activity 2.8

Switching Between Windows

1. You now have the Clock and the Calculator running. Restore the Clock.

    double-click the Clock icon

    You can now see both windows open on the screen at the same time.

2. Switch between windows.

    click in the Calculator window

    click in the Clock window

    Notice that the title bar of the active window is emphasized.

3. Switch to a third window.

    click in the Program Manager window

    Did the Clock or the Calculator disappear behind the Program Manager?

4. Redisplay the Clock and Calculator windows, then minimize them.

    minimize the Program Manager window

    minimize the Clock and the Calculator

    double-click the Program Manager icon

    You should now have the Program Manager window open on the screen with the Clock and Calculator running as icons on the desktop.

The Calendar Program

The Calendar accessory provides a handy way to schedule appointments and make reminders for yourself. In this section, you'll work with the Calendar program. While doing so, you'll learn about using pull-down menus and dialog boxes, and you'll see how to open and save files.

The picture below shows two ways — daily and monthly — that the Calendar program might be displayed.

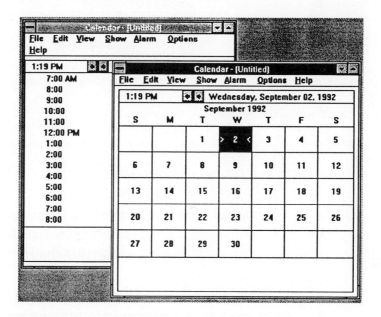

Activity 2.9 | Starting the Calendar Program

1. From the Accessories group, run the Calendar program.

   double-click the Calendar icon

2. Maximize the program.

   select the maximize button

Using Pull-Down Menus

Pull-down menus are the way that Windows provides command choices. Using a pull-down menu is a two-step process.

- Pull down a menu by selecting its name in the menu bar.

- Choose a command by selecting it from the pull-down menu.

Note: Throughout this book, the two-step process for selecting commands from menus will be represented like this:

select File, New

This means you should select the word File from the menu bar and then select the word New from the pull-down menu.

If you change your mind about choosing a command from a menu, you can stop the process by closing the menu.

- Close the menu by clicking anywhere else in the window or pressing [Esc].

Once you have pulled down a menu, you may notice some differences among command choices. For example, you may not be able to select some commands.

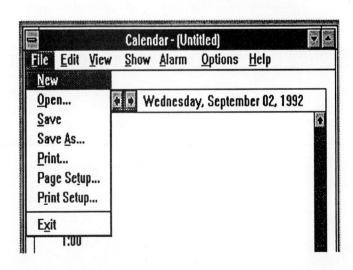

- Commands that are "grayed" or "dimmed" are not available for current use.

Once selected, some commands will execute immediately; others will ask for additional information.

- Commands that require additional information are followed by an ellipsis (...) on the menu.

When you choose one of these commands, a dialog box will appear.

In the next section you'll learn how to use a menu choice and dialog box to open a Calendar file.

Opening Files

Right now you have an empty calendar on the screen. The program title bar lists the calendar as [Untitled]. You could begin to enter appointments in this calendar and then save the calendar as a file on disk. Once you've saved a calendar as a file, you open that file each time you want to make alterations (e.g., add an appointment or change one).

Opening a file means that the program reads the file from disk into memory. Once the file is in memory, you can work with it. When you're finished, you save your changes to the disk.

A program is capable of handling many files. You might have several calendars that you'd like to use. For example, you might have a business calendar, a calendar of birthdays you want to remember, and a social calendar. You might even want to keep individual calendars for different members of your family. Each of your calendars can be saved on disk as a separate file.

- Files are opened and saved through the File pull-down menu and associated dialog boxes.

- The first time you save a file you must give it a name.

- The file extension for calendar files is .CAL.

The procedure for opening and saving files is the same in most Windows applications.

- To open a file, you select File, Open from the menu. When you do so, the File Open dialog box appears.

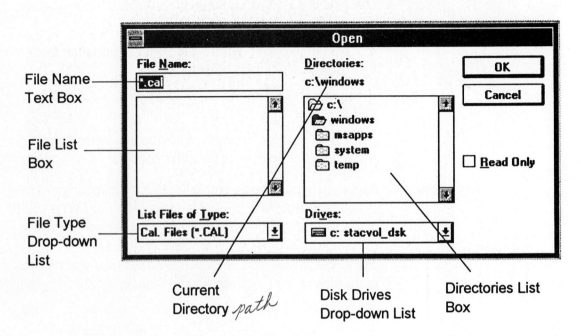

File Name Text Box

File List Box

File Type Drop-down List

Current Directory *path*

Disk Drives Drop-down List

Directories List Box

Activity 2.10 | **Opening a File**

Before beginning this activity, place your student diskette in the A: drive. If you're using a different disk drive, substitute its letter (e.g., B:) when working with this and other activities.

1. Begin the File Open process.

select File, Open

In the File Open dialog box, the File Name text box looks for files ending in the .CAL extension. Any files that match the List Files of Type are shown in the list box below the File Name text box.

The current disk drive is shown in the Drives drop-down list; the current directory is shown above the Directories list box.

If the file you wish to open resides on a different disk drive or directory than the current directory, you must select that drive and/or directory.

2. Open a Calendar file from the student diskette in drive A:.

click the down arrow for the Drives list

click the A: drive

click BUSY.CAL in the files list

click the OK button

The file is read from disk into memory. Its name appears in the title bar of the program window.

Activity 2.11 ## Changing the Interval Setting

Look at the calendar displayed on your screen. Notice that the schedule is set to show appointments at one-hour intervals. You'll use a menu choice and dialog box to change to fifteen-minute intervals.

1. Choose a pull-down menu in the Calendar menu bar.

select Options

2. Note that the Day Settings command is followed by an ellipsis.

select Day Settings

The Day Settings dialog box appears.

Day Settings	
Interval: ○ 15 ○ 30 ◉ 60	
Hour Format: ◉ 12 ○ 24	**OK**
Starting Time: 7:00 AM	**Cancel**

3.   Choose a 15-minute interval.

click the 15-minute option button

The option button showing the current choice has a dark center.

4.   Confirm your selection.

click the OK button

Look at the calendar to see if the appointment interval has changed.

On Your Own

1.   Change the view of the calendar from a daily to monthly calendar by selecting View, Month from the menu bar.

2.   There are two arrows in the Time and Date bar above the calendar. What do they do?

3.   What happens if you double-click the date in the Time and Date bar?

4.   Now what do the arrows do?

5.   How is today's date marked on the month view?

Activity 2.12

Using the Scroll Bar

1.   Return to the daily view of the calendar.

select View, Day

2.   Move through the appointment schedule with the Up and Down scroll arrows.

click the down scroll arrow

click the down scroll arrow two times in succession

3.   Browse through the schedule.

click and hold down the mouse button on the down scroll arrow

What happens to the scroll box as you browse through the schedule?

4. Center the scroll box.

click up or down until the scroll box is centered in the scroll bar

5. Move a page at a time.

click in the scroll bar above or below the scroll box

What happens?

6. Move to the top and bottom of the schedule.

drag the scroll box to the top of the scroll bar

drag the scroll box to the bottom of the scroll bar

Moving to a Specific Date

You're interested in looking at the calendar schedule for 6/19/92 to see what your appointments were for that day. You could move to the date month-by-month and day-by-day, but there's an easier way. You can type in the desired date in a text box within a dialog box. To begin, you select Show, Date from the menu. The Show Date dialog box opens.

In the Show Date dialog box, the insertion point is in the text box where you're to type the date you wish to display.

If highlighted (white text on a dark background) text is present in the box, typing will replace that text.

There are two buttons in the dialog box — OK and Cancel. The default button has an emphasized border. You can click either button; or, if you want the default button, you can press [Enter].

Activity 2.13

Finding a Date

1. Look for a particular date.

   select Show, Date

2. The cursor is positioned within the text box.

   type 6/19/92

   press [Enter] or click the OK button

   The calendar shows the proper date.

3. Note the appointments for the day.

   scroll through the schedule

   How many appointments were there?

4. Check the monthly calendar to see if any dates are marked.

   select View, Month

5. Look at the schedule for the marked day.

Entering Text

The text cursor is a blinking vertical line called the *insertion point*. It is positioned at the point where text will be entered.

If you move your mouse pointer around on the Calendar, you'll notice that it's sometimes shaped like an I-beam. The I-beam shows the position of the mouse within a text area.

Clicking when the I-beam cursor is within a text area will move the insertion point to that position.

You may add appointments by clicking next to the desired time, then typing in the text that describes the appointment. If you make mistakes while typing, press [Backspace] and correct them.

On Your Own

1. Move to a day next week.

2. Type in a breakfast meeting and an afternoon appointment for that day.

3. Click in the large text box at the bottom of the calendar.

4. Type **Call Joe** there.

5. Go to the month view. Is the text there as well?

Activity 2.14

Saving a File

You've now made several changes to your calendar. Those changes exist only in the copy of the file that is in the memory of your computer. In this activity, you'll save the changes to the file on disk.

1. Save the calendar.

   select File, Save

   Note: The mouse pointer changes to an hourglass while the program is working. While this pointer is displayed, you should not press any keys or click the mouse button.

2. Prepare for the next activity.

   select File, New

Activity 2.15

Creating Your Own Calendar

1. Go to the calendar page for the first day of next month.

2. Add a 9:00 AM appointment.

   type EARLY MEETING WITH MR. WILSON

3. Mark the day with symbol 1 on the monthly calendar.

select Options, Mark

choose Symbol 1 in the dialog box

click OK

Saving Your New Calendar

When you want to save a file for the first time, you must provide a name for the file. Windows file names must obey DOS conventions:

- The name must be from one to eight alphanumeric characters in length.

- Spaces and most punctuation characters are not allowed. You may use the hyphen (-) or the underscore (_).

- The .CAL extension is automatically added to the file name by the Calendar program.

Activity 2.16

Naming and Saving a File

1. Save the calendar.

   select File, Save as

   type the file name MYMTGS in the File, Save As dialog box

2. Save the file.

   click OK

On Your Own

1. Create a new calendar file for your social engagements.

2. Add a few items to next weekend to reflect your social schedule.

3. Mark the 28th on next month's calendar.

4. Type a note to yourself in the text box at the bottom of the calendar for that day.

5. Save the calendar with the name SOCIAL and minimize the Calendar window.

Quick Check

1. How do you start a program?

2. Describe how to size a window.

3. Describe how to move a window.

4. To select a command from a pull-down menu, you

   _____

   _____.

5. Answer the following questions true or false.

   _____Commands that are followed by an ellipsis
   execute immediately.

   _____Commands that are grayed are unavailable.

   _____You can close a menu by pressing [Esc].

6. Before you can work with a file from disk, you must
   _____ it.

7. If you want to keep changes to a file, you must
   _____ the file.

Chapter
3

More Desktop Accessories

Overview

In this chapter, you'll learn how to transfer text from one
Windows application to another through the technique of
cutting and pasting. You'll be able to run several programs
at the same time and conveniently switch between them.
Also, you'll become familiar with two additional Windows
accessories, the Notepad and the Cardfile.

Objectives

- Enter and edit text in the Notepad

- Select text

- Cut, copy, and paste to rearrange text

- Access the Cardfile

- Add a card

- Search for a card

- Cut, copy, and paste from Cardfile to Notepad

- Switch between multiple applications

Entering Text in the Notepad

The Notepad accessory program is a simple word processor. It is used to produce ASCII text files. Such files may contain simple text — letters, numbers, punctuation, and spaces — but no underlining, bolding, or other formatting codes. The Notepad is useful for notes and simple memos. You may also find it valuable for producing and editing DOS batch files. With the Notepad, you can:

- Save and retrieve documents
- Use full screen editing (move the cursor anywhere in the text area)
- Cut and paste
- Search for text
- Print a document

Activity 3.1 | Starting Notepad

1. Start the Notepad from the Accessories program group.

   open the Accessories group
   double-click the Notepad
   maximize the program window

2. Observe the mouse pointer.

   move the mouse pointer around the text area
   move the mouse pointer into the title and menu bars

   What is the appearance of the mouse pointer in the text area? In other areas?

Cursor and Pointer

In the text area of the Notepad, you should see two cursors:

- The flashing vertical bar is the text insertion point — the position where text will be entered as you begin to type.

- The I-beam shows the position of the mouse pointer within the text area.

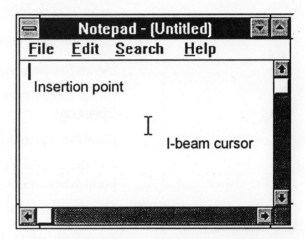

You can move the insertion point within the text area by using the cursor direction keys. You can also move the insertion point by positioning the I-beam cursor within the text and clicking the mouse button.

Entering and Editing Text

There are some simple rules for entering text within the Notepad.

- When typing text in the Notepad, end each line of text by pressing the [Enter] key.

- If you make a mistake, use the [Backspace] key to erase the last characters you typed to the left of the insertion point.

- To delete characters at the insertion point or to the right of it, use the [Delete] key.

Activity 3.2	**Opening a Notepad File**

1. Retrieve a Notepad file.

select File, Open

click the down arrow for the Drives list

click the A: drive

double-click TODOLIST.TXT in the list of files

2. Move the insertion point.

move the I-beam to the second line of text

move the I-beam to the space after the word Tuesday

click the mouse button

Did the insertion point move? Leave the insertion point where it is.

3. Insert text into the document.

type Saturday

What happened to the rest of the text in the line as you typed?

4. Delete text from the document.

press the [Backspace] until the word Saturday is gone

What happened to the rest of the text in the line?

Selecting Text

It's awkward to use the backspace to delete or erase large blocks of text. These changes may be handled by first highlighting or marking the text and then deleting it. Highlighted text appears in inverse video, that is, white letters on black background.

There are three methods of highlighting.

Highlighting with the mouse

Move the I-beam (mouse) cursor to the beginning of the block to be highlighted and hold down the mouse button.

Drag the I-beam to the end of the block.

Release the mouse button.

Highlighting with the keyboard

Move the flashing insertion point to the beginning of the block to be highlighted.

Hold down the [Shift] key.

With the [Shift] key held down, use the arrow keys on the keyboard to move to the end of the block.

Release the [Shift] key.

Highlighting with the mouse and the keyboard

Move the insertion point to the beginning of the block to be highlighted. Move the I-beam mouse cursor to the end of the block.

Hold down the [Shift] key and click the mouse button.

Activity 3.3

Highlighting Text

1. Highlight by dragging.

   drag the I-beam cursor over the first line of text

2. Remove the highlighting.

   click the I-beam cursor somewhere else

3. Highlight with the cursor.

   move the insertion point to the beginning of the second list

   press and hold down the [Shift] key

   use the arrow keys to move the cursor to the end of the list

   release the [Shift] key

4. Remove the highlighting.

   move the insertion point with a cursor key

5. Highlight with the [Shift] key and mouse.

   move the insertion point to the beginning of the

first list

move the I-beam cursor to the end of the second list

press and hold down the [Shift] key

click the mouse button

Cut, Copy, and Paste

Once text has been selected or highlighted, you may *cut, copy,* or *delete* it.

- **Cut** removes the highlighted text from the screen but places it in a special area of memory called the Clipboard for possible later use.

- **Copy** keeps the text on the screen and places a copy of it in a special area of memory called the Clipboard for possible later use.

- **Delete** erases the text from the screen but does not keep it in special memory.

Once text has been cut or copied, you can *paste* it somewhere else. You can also *undo* the cut, copy, delete, or paste.

- **Undo** allows you to change your mind about the most recent cut, copy, or delete.

- **Paste** retrieves the cut or copied text. The pasted text will appear at the flashing insertion point.

  Note: Only the most recently cut or copied text can be pasted. You may paste as many copies from memory as you wish.

Activity 3.4

Basic Cut and Paste

1. Cut text from the document.

   highlight the first list

   select Edit, Cut from the menu

   What happened to the text?

2. Paste text back into the document. Don't move the

insertion point.

select Edit, Paste

Did the text reappear? Why were you asked not to move the insertion point?

Activity 3.5 | Moving Text with Cut and Paste

1. Prepare the second list for moving.

    highlight the second list

2. Remove the list.

    select Edit, Cut

3. Move the insertion point.

    place the insertion point at the beginning of the first list

4. Paste the cut list onto the screen.

    select Edit, Paste

Activity 3.6 | Copying Text

1. Edit the text so you're ready to begin next week's list.

    highlight Monday, Tuesday, Wednesday

2. Copy the paragraph into memory.

    select Edit, Copy

3. Move to the end of the document.

    place the insertion point at the end of the document

4. Paste the copy from memory.

    select Edit, Paste

    Note that Cut, Copy, and Delete commands are

grayed, so they aren't options you can choose.

5. Remove the copy.

   select Edit, Undo

6. Save the Notepad file with a new name.

   select File, Save As
   *type **MEMO1** in the file name text box*
   click the OK button

On Your Own

1. Use cut and paste to put the list items in correct order.

2. Put a copy of the first list at the end of the document.

3. Save the file.

4. Minimize the Notepad.

The Cardfile

The Cardfile accessory allows you to keep track of information on electronic index cards. You can, for example, keep a handy list of names and addresses that you'd otherwise keep in a manual card file ready for use.

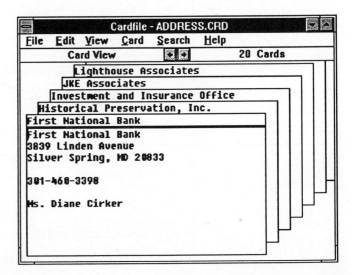

Each card consists of an **index line** and an **address area**. The index line is used for sorting and searching; the address area is general use. With the Cardfile you may:

- Create an electronic file of index cards.

- Keep the cards in alphabetical order by index.

- View the cards or a list of index entries.

- Search for items in the index list.

Activity 3.7

Opening a Cardfile

1. Open the Cardfile program.

   double-click Cardfile in the Accessories group

2. Open a file on the A: drive.

   select File, Open
   click the down arrow for the Drives list
   click the A: drive
   double-click ADDRESS.CRD in the list of files

3. Select a view and look through the Cardfile entries.

   select View, List
   select View, Card

4. Browse through the entries.

   click right and left arrow buttons
   select View, List
   click right and left arrow buttons

Activity 3.8

Adding a Card

1. Change to the card view.

   select View, Card

2. Add a card.

select Card, Add

type your name (last name, first name) in the Add text box

select the OK button

You've just added an index line. Now you need to fill in the card.

3. Fill in the card.

type your name, address, and phone number

Activity 3.9 **Finding a Card**

1. Find the card that contains the name "Baker."

select Search, Find

type **Baker**

click Find Next

2. Close the Find window

double-click the Control Menu box

There are several cards that contain the word "Baker." Suppose this isn't the one you want.

3. Find the next card that contains the name "Baker."

select Search, Find Next

Did you notice that next to the Find Next menu choice was the notation "F3"? This is the keyboard shortcut for that menu choice.

4. Use the keyboard shortcut to find the next card that contains the name "Baker."

press [F3]

On Your Own

1. How would you change an entry in the address area? Try changing your address from home to work or school.

2. Can you cut, copy, and paste in a Cardfile? Try to copy a phone number from one card to another.

3. Delete your card from the Cardfile.

Transferring Text

When text is cut or copied, it's placed in a special place in memory called the Clipboard where it becomes available for pasting. You've seen how this works within a single application like the Notepad. In the next activity, you'll take advantage of this Windows feature to transfer text from the Cardfile to the Clipboard.

Activity 3.10

Cutting into the Clipboard

1. Open the Cardfile program and retrieve the ADDRESS.CRD file if necessary.

2. Copy from the Cardfile program.

   find the Outreach Computers entry

   highlight the entire address entry

   select Edit, Copy

   click the Cardfile minimize button

3. Start the Notepad and paste into it.

   double-click the Notepad icon

   select Edit, Paste

   Did the text you copied from the Cardfile appear in the Notepad?

4. Minimize the Notepad.

   click the Notepad minimize button

Switching Between Applications

Sometimes your screen desktop can get disorganized like your real desktop. Until now, you've mostly been working with one program at a time and minimizing the window to put it aside. As you begin working with more programs, you may not remember where things are, or a program icon may disappear behind another window. Also, you may want to switch quickly from one program to another.

The Task List

The purpose of the Task List is to provide an escape valve when your desktop gets too cluttered, and you begin to lose things. When you open the task list, you'll see a list of all the programs that are currently running. There are several ways to get to the Task List:

- Press [Ctrl][Esc].

  OR

- Double-click anywhere on the desktop outside any window.

  OR

- Select Control menu, Switch To.

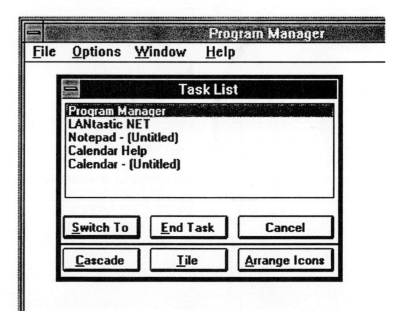

From the Task List, you can quickly switch to a program by double-clicking its name in the list. Or, click the button for the action you want to perform.

- The **Switch To** button switches control to the selected program.

- The **End Task** button closes the selected program.

- **Cascade** and **Tile** arrange open program windows.

- **Arrange Icons** rearranges the icons which represent minimized programs.

Activity 3.11

Using the Task List

To start this activity, you should have the Program Manager window on your screen with the Notepad and Cardfile programs running and minimized as icons on the desktop.

1. Minimize the Program Manager.

   click the minimize button

2. Start Task List.

   double-click on the desktop

   Notice that the Task List shows all the programs that are currently running.

3. Switch to the Cardfile program.

   select Cardfile in the Task List
   click the Switch To button

4. Start Task List again and switch to the Notepad.

   press [Ctrl][Esc]
   double-click Notepad in the Task List

5. Start Task List again and rearrange the open Windows.

   press [Ctrl][Esc]
   select the Tile button

6.   Start Task List again and try a different arrangement.

press [Ctrl][Esc]
select Cascade

7.   Restore the Program Manager window.

double-click the Program Manager icon

Switching Between Programs

You've seen how the Task List lets you switch programs. It's also possible to switch directly from one program to the next. There are two main methods:

- Press [Alt][Esc] to move to the next program window.
  OR

- Press [Alt][Tab] to cycle through each program that is running.

When you press [Alt][Tab], the name and icon for the next program appear in a small window in the center of the screen. To move to the next program, continue to hold the [Alt] key down, while pressing [Tab]. When you see the name and icon for the program you want to work with, release the [Alt] key. The selected program will be made active.

Activity 3.12

Switching Between Programs

1.   With the Notepad, Cardfile, and Program Manager all running, switch to the next program.

press [Alt][Esc] to reach the next program
continue with [Alt][Esc] through all the programs

2.   Try the faster method for cycling through the available programs.

press [Alt][Tab] to reach the next program
continue holding [Alt] while pressing [Tab]
when the desired program appears, release [Alt]

On Your Own

1. Open the Notepad and the Cardfile and arrange them for easy viewing.

2. Practice copying back and forth between the Notepad and Cardfile.

3. Close the Notepad and the Cardfile.

Quick Check

1. The Notepad is used to create what type of files?

2. Describe two ways of selecting text in the Notepad.

3. List the four steps for moving text in the Notepad.

4. What is the difference between Cut and Copy?

5. How do you add a card in the Cardfile?

6. Can you copy and paste between the Notepad and the Cardfile? How?

7. List three ways to start the Task List.

Chapter
4

Other Accessories and Techniques

Overview

You've seen how you can create documents with the Notepad and how you can share text between applications. Now, you'll create documents with more attractive text formatting, as well as create and transfer graphics.

In addition, you'll work with special characters, such as copyright symbols, bullets, or foreign letters with accents. Such special characters are a cross between graphics and text, and you can use them in many Windows programs.

To see how text can be formatted and how graphics can be created and transferred, you'll use two application programs that are furnished with Windows: Write and Paintbrush. Write is a word processing program that provides some of the features found in more expensive word processors. Paintbrush is a graphics program that lets you create original pictures or edit existing graphics. You'll also use the Character Map accessory to include special characters in your documents.

When you've learned some of the basic techniques used in programs like Write and Paintbrush, you'll automate some of the more repetitive procedures by writing macros. Then, you'll be able to quickly perform some of your most frequently needed tasks.

Objectives

- Edit and format a document with the Write accessory program

- Use fonts to enhance text

- Print a document

- View the special characters available with the Character Map

- Copy special characters into a Write document

- Draw simple figures with Paintbrush

- Add text to graphics

- Paste a graphic into a document

- Automate procedures using the Macro Recorder

- Utilize a macro in both Write and Notepad

Using Write as a Word Processor

You've already mastered the basics of word processing — you did this when you studied the Notepad. In this chapter you'll learn to use a more sophisticated word processor, Windows Write. With Write you can:

- Type text without pressing [Enter] at the end of each line.

- Set tabs and paragraph indents.

- Center and justify text.

- Use bold, italics, and underlining for emphasis.

- Use various fonts and character sizes.

- Add graphics to your document.

In fact, Write has many of the features included with more powerful (and expensive) word processing programs. One feature that is not included is a spelling checker. So be sure to proofread your documents carefully!

In this section it's assumed that you already know most of the techniques used in Windows word processing. These essentials include:

- Using the [Backspace] or [Delete] keys to erase text.

- Moving around in text with the cursor direction keys.

- Moving the mouse cursor and insertion point.

- Highlighting blocks of text.

- Cutting, copying, and pasting text.

If you've forgotten how to perform any of these tasks, review the section on the Notepad accessory program (Chapter 3) before continuing with this chapter.

Activity 4.1   ## Starting Write

1. Open the Write program window.

double-click the Write icon in the Accessories program group.

Look at the Write program window. The screen looks much like the Notepad. The text and I-beam cursors appear as they did in Notepad, but the Write screen has a Page number in the lower left-hand corner of the window and several new menu commands. Also note the end-of-document mark, a small circle with four short radiating lines.

2. Retrieve a file from the student diskette.

select File, Open

click the down arrow for the Drives list

click the A: drive

double-click ACME.WRI in the files list

Write documents use a .WRI extension.

Formatting

You can apply formatting to characters by boldfacing, italicizing, or underlining them. Or, for an even bigger difference, you can change the font and size of text characters.

You can also format paragraphs to be centered, left- or right-aligned, or justified. And, you can indent paragraphs in several ways.

In the next activities, you're going to use the formatting features in Write to change the appearance of your document.

Activity 4.2

Character Formatting

1. Add a sentence. (Do *not* press [Enter] at the end of each line; only at the end of a paragraph.)

    before the last paragraph, add the paragraph "We have been doing business continually in the Nebraska/Iowa area since 1925."

    Did you notice how the line wrapped down to the next line as you typed past the right margin?

2. Add bold to words.

    highlight "ACME UNIFORM SERVICE" at the bottom of the first paragraph

    select Character, Bold

    to view the bold formatting, click somewhere else on the screen

3. Add an underline to a word. To highlight a word, double-click the I-beam cursor within the word.

double-click the word "great" in the first line of the second paragraph

select Character, Underline

4. Add italics to the paragraph beginning with ''We at ACME UNIFORM SERVICE.... ''

move the I-beam cursor into the left margin so that it becomes an arrow

move the arrow alongside the paragraph to be highlighted

double-click

select Character, Italic

Note: Depending on the font you're using, you may not see italics. Some fonts, such as Courier, aren't available in italics.

Activity 4.3

Paragraph Formatting

1. Provide a first line indent for a paragraph.

highlight all the paragraphs in the body of the letter

select Paragraph, Indents

in the First Line text box of the Indents dialog box, type **.25**

click the OK button

Each highlighted paragraph now has a .25" indent.

2. Indent a paragraph on both sides.

move the insertion point into the paragraph beginning with "We at ACME UNIFORM SERVICE...."

select Paragraph, Indent

type **1"** *into the Left Indent text box*

type 0" into the First Line text box

type 1" into the Right Indent text box

click the OK button

Fonts

You may change the type style or font used in your document. A number of different type styles come with the Windows program, and they can be used on any printer. You may have more font choices than the ones mentioned in this exercise.

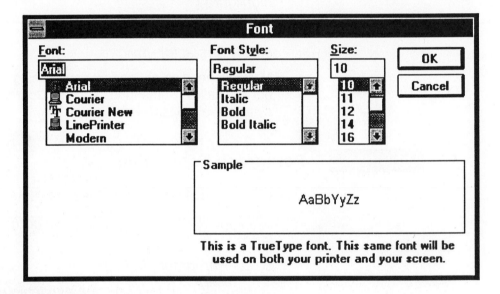

Activity 4.4 **Changing Fonts**

1. Highlight the entire document.

    move the I-beam cursor into the left margin

    when the cursor becomes a rightward-pointing arrow, hold down the [Ctrl] key and click the mouse button

2. Change the font.

    select Character, Fonts and choose Arial

    click the OK button

Activity 4.5

Character Map

Printing

1. Print the document.

   select File, Print

2. Note the defaults and print.

   click OK

On Your Own

1. Highlight the entire document.

2. Select Character, Fonts to see what other fonts are available.

3. Select a different font.

4. Print the document.

5. Save the document and minimize the Write program.

The Character Map accessory displays the many characters that are available for use in Windows programs. These characters include mathematical symbols, foreign alphabets, and graphical symbols such as stars, bullets, and arrows.

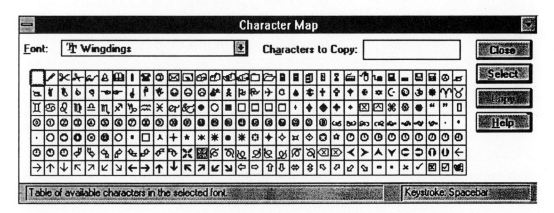

The symbols can be copied from the Character Map to Write and other Windows programs.

Activity 4.6	**Viewing Special Characters**

1. Open the Character Map program in the Accessories group.

   double-click the Character Map icon

2. Pick a set of characters to view.

   click the down arrow next to the name of the font
   scroll to the top of the list
   select Arial from the list of fonts

3. View the first character on the second line, an "at" symbol @.

   point to the @ and hold down the mouse button

4. View some of the other characters.

   point and hold the mouse button on several of the characters in the map

5. View the Wingdings character set.

   click the down arrow next to the name of the font
   scroll to the bottom of the list
   select Wingdings from the list of fonts
   point and hold the mouse button on several of the characters in the map

Activity 4.7	**Copying Special Characters to Write**

1. Select the telephone symbol from the Wingdings character set.

   click the telephone character
   click the Select button

2. Copy the character to the clipboard.

   click the Copy button

3. Open the Write program.

    double-click the Write icon

4. Paste the telephone character.

    choose Edit, Paste

    Don't worry if the result doesn't look like a telephone. This is because the Wingdings font may not be the currently selected font in Write.

5. Change the font and size of the pasted item.

    highlight the pasted symbol with the mouse

    choose Character, Fonts

    select the Wingdings font

    select a 26 point size

    click the OK button

    The telephone character should now be showing.

On Your Own

1. Copy the registered trademark symbol ® from the Times New Roman Character Map.

2. Paste it into your Write document.

3. Highlight it and select the Times New Roman font with a 16 point size.

4. If there is a printer available, print the document.

Using Paintbrush to Create Graphics

In addition to a word processor, Windows also comes with a graphics or paint program that allows you to draw anything from simple logos to rather complex works of art. Windows Paintbrush gives you facilities to:

*   Draw lines, curves, boxes and circles.

*   Fill enclosed spaces with color.

- Add text to graphics.
- Cut and paste.
- Spray on color.
- Edit graphics.

Look at the drawing screen below. Along the left side of the window is the toolbox. You select a tool by clicking its icon. The tools are described on the following page.

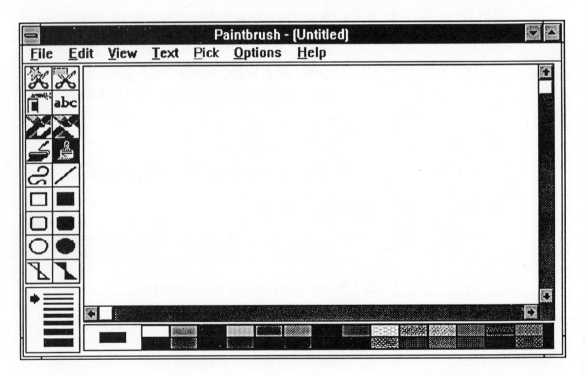

The Toolbox

The **Scissors** tool is used to select an irregularly shaped area to cut or copy			The **Pick** tool is used to select a rectangular area to cut or copy
The **Airbrush** tool is used to create spray-paint effects			The **Text** tool lets you enter text on your graphic
The **Color Eraser** is used to change a figure's foreground color			The **Eraser** is used to rub out the foreground color
The **Paint Roller** is used to fill enclosed shapes with the foreground color			The **Paintbrush** is used to draw freehand shapes
The **Curve** tool is used to turn straight lines into smooth curves			The **Line** tool is used to draw lines
The **Open Box** tool is used to create hollow squares and rectangles			The **Filled Box** tool is used to create squares and rectangles filled with the foreground color
The **Open Rounded Box** tool is used to create hollow rounded squares and rectangles			The **Filled Rounded Box** tool is used to create rounded squares and rectangles filled with the foreground color
The **Open Circle/Ellipse** tool is used to create hollow circles and ellipses			The **Filled Circle/Ellipse** tool is used to create circles and ellipses filled with the foreground color
The **Open Polygon** tool is used to create hollow, irregular closed shapes			The **Filled Polygon** tool is used to create filled, irregular closed shapes

Drawing Basics

The general process of drawing involves the following steps:

- Select a drawing tool. This might be the straight line, curve, or even an open box rectangle tool.

- Choose a line width from the selection shown below the toolbox.

- Choose a foreground color. Click a color in the palette along the bottom of the Paintbrush window. The color appears at the center of the color box at the left end of the palette.

- Choose a background color. Click the *right* mouse button on a color in the palette. The color appears as a border around the foreground color in the color box. (Some tools don't use a background color.)

When you are ready, draw by dragging the cursor from one location to another. The results will depend on which tool you're using. When you begin to draw somewhere else, the original object is pasted down.

You may select Edit, Undo to erase the last object drawn.

Activity 4.8

Practice Drawing

1. Open Paintbrush.

    double-click Paintbrush

2. Draw boxes.

    select the open box tool
    select a line width

3. Select a foreground and background color.

    click the left mouse button on the desired foreground color

    click the right mouse button on the desired background color

4. Draw two boxes.

hold down the left mouse button and drag the cursor to draw a small box

select the filled box tool

hold down the left mouse button and drag the cursor to draw a second small box

Note the difference in the way the foreground and background colors work with the box tools.

5. Clear the screen.

select white as the background color and black as the foreground color

select File, New

select No in the caution box to throw away the old drawing

6. Draw with the line tool.

select the line tool

select a line width and foreground color

hold down the left mouse button and drag the cursor to draw a line

Note the difference in lines if you hold down the Shift key while drawing.

On Your Own

1. Practice drawing ellipses and circles with the circle tool.

2. See if you can draw a wave like an S with the curve tool. Try dragging on first one side of the line and then on the other.

Activity 4.9

More Paintbrush Tools

1. Airbrush a line.

select the airbrush tool

draw a line with the airbrush

The airbrush tool works with foreground colors and the line widths. Try different combinations. Results with the air brush also depend on how fast you move the mouse. Try different dragging speeds.

2. Paint a line.

select the paintbrush

draw a line with the paintbrush

How does the paintbrush differ from the airbrush? You may also select a paintbrush thickness with the line width choice.

3. Fill a shape with the paint roller.

select File, New to erase the screen

select No to lose your present graphic

create a filled box with your choice of colors

select the paint roller tool

select a different foreground color

move the cursor inside the box and click the mouse button

The paint roller fills an enclosed area with the foreground color.

Activity 4.10 Erasing

1. Erase an area.

select the (right) eraser tool

choose a line width to select the size of the eraser

select white as a background color

drag the eraser across a part of the filled box

The eraser erases with the background color.

2. Erase a color.

clear or erase the screen

select one of the middle line widths

select green as a foreground color and red as a background color

draw a filled box with 3" sides

select the color (left) eraser

select blue as a background color

drag the color eraser across the box

| Activity 4.11 | ## Cutting and Copying |

To begin this activity, reset foreground color to black and background color to white.

1. Clear the screen and draw a box.

select File, New to erase the screen

select No to lose your present graphic

draw a large filled box with your choice of colors

2. Cut away a part of the box with the scissors (left scissors tool).

select the scissors tool

move the cursor inside the perimeter of the box

drag the cursor in a small figure-eight pattern

select Edit, Cut

The scissors tool is used to cut an irregular hole in an object so that the background color shows through.

3. Cut a rectangular area with the pick (right scissors) tool.

select the pick tool

move the cursor to the upper right-hand corner of the filled box drag the cursor down and to the left to create an outline covering one quarter of the filled box

select Edit, Cut

The pick tool is used to cut a regular, rectangular area.

4. Paste the cut material back onto the graphic.

   select Edit, Paste

   drag the pasted section back into place

Adding Text

You may also add text to your drawing. Choose the text tool, a font, style and size, and then type from the position of the cursor.

Note: You can backspace if you make a mistake *while typing*. However, once you click your cursor in a new location on the screen, the text becomes just another graphical element of your picture, and you will no longer be able to edit the typed text!

Activity 4.12

Adding a Line of Text

1. Type text into your picture

   select blue as the foreground color

   select the text tool (the ABC tool next to the spray can)

   select Text, Fonts, Times New Roman

   select Style, Bold

   select Size, 36

   click OK

   click the cursor near the left edge of the drawing area

   *type **WINDOWS PAINTBRUSH***

   While you're still typing, you may change the font, size, and style. All the text in the current line will change.

Pasting a Graphic

Just as you transferred text from the Cardfile to a Notepad document, you can also transfer graphics between Paintbrush and Write. The steps are:

- Open Paintbrush.

- Retrieve or draw the graphic you want to export to Write.

- Use the pick tool to copy the graphic to the Clipboard.

- Open Write and create or retrieve the file that is to receive the graphic.

- Position the insertion point where the graphic is to appear.

- Paste the graphic from the Clipboard.

Activity 4.13

Pasting a Graphic into Write

1. Start the Paintbrush program if necessary. Retrieve the graphic.

    select File, Open

    click the down arrow for the Drives list

    click the A: drive

    double-click LOGO.BMP in the list of files

2. Copy the DSR logo to the Clipboard. *rectangular to cutor copy*

    select the pick tool

    if necessary, scroll to get the entire logo on screen

    draw an outline around the entire logo

    select Edit, Copy

    The logo has now been copied to the Clipboard.

3. Open Write and retrieve a file.

    restore the Write program

select File, Open

click the down arrow for the Drives list

click the A: drive

double-click TEXT.WRI

4. Paste the logo into the document.

    move the insertion to the top left position in the document

    select Edit, Paste

5. Quit the Paintbrush program.

    double-click the Paintbrush Control-menu box

    click the No button

6. Quit the Write Program

    double-click the Write Control-menu box

    click the No button

On Your Own

1. You may size and move a graphic after it's been inserted into Write. Click the logo and use Edit, Size Picture to reduce it to half size. This procedure works a little differently than the sizing you've done before. You may want to read the Help entry on sizing pictures.

2. Print the document if you have a printer attached.

The Recorder

The recorder works like a tape recorder. It's used to make a record of the steps required for a frequently used procedure, such as signing a letter or setting up a memo form. Later, this "tape recording," or **macro**, can be played back to automate the procedure.

You can have several files or "sets" of macros. For example, if several people share a computer, each user can create a file of his or her macros. Each file could then contain a signature macro for the appropriate user. If you want to use macros again in a future work session, you must save them in a file.

With the macro recorder, you can:

• Assign a name to a commonly used procedure.

• Record the steps in the procedure.

• Play the steps back with simple shortcut keys.

• Save the macros in a file for future use.

Some macros can even be replayed in programs other than those in which they were recorded, provided the steps work the same way in both programs.

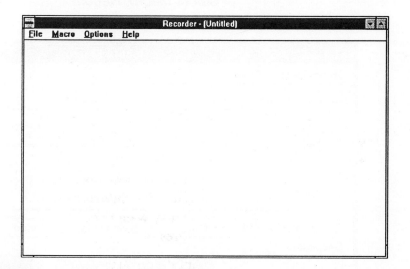

Activity 4.14 ## Recording a Macro

1. If necessary, close any open programs, then start the Write Program in a non-maximized window.

    double-click the Write icon in the Accessories group

    if necessary, size the window to leave 1" of desktop visible at the bottom of your screen

2. Switch back to the Accessories window.

   press [Alt][Tab] until the Program Manager becomes active

3. Open the Recorder and minimize the Program Manager.

   double-click the Recorder icon in the Accessories group

   press [Alt][Tab] until the Program Manager becomes active

   click the Program Manager's minimize button

4. In the Recorder window, begin recording a macro.

   select Macro, Record

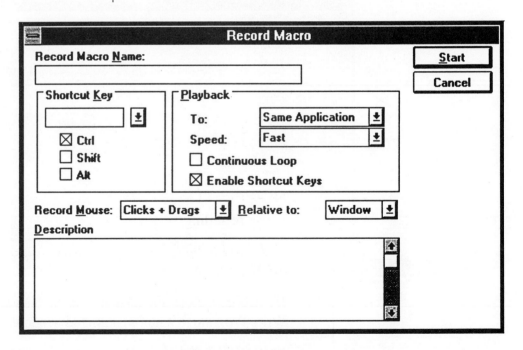

5. Name the macro and select [Ctrl][S] as the shortcut keys for future playback.

   type SIGNATURE

press [Tab] to reach the Shortcut Key section

type **S**

make sure there is an X in the box for the Ctrl key

6. Specify that this macro can be played back in other applications besides Write.

   in the Playback section, click the down arrow next to "Same Application"

   select Any Application

7. Tell the recorder to ignore movements of the mouse.

   click the down arrow next to "Clicks + Drags"

   select Ignore Mouse

8. Begin recording.

   click Start

9. With the cursor flashing in the Write document, carefully type your signature block. (If you make mistakes, they will be recorded as well.)

   type **Sincerely yours,**

   press [Enter] several times

   type your name

   press [Enter]

10. Finish recording.

    click the flashing Recorder icon at the bottom of the desktop

    click the OK button in the dialogue box

    You have now finished recording the macro.

| Activity 4.15 | **Playing Back a Macro** |

1. Clear the screen in Write.

select File, New

click NO to lose changes

2. Play the signature macro.

press [Ctrl][S]

3. Close Write, and test the macro in the Notepad program.

double-click the Write Control-menu box

click NO to lose the changes

double-click the Notepad icon

press [Ctrl][S]

Does the signature block appear properly here?

| Activity 4.16 | **Recording a Longer Macro** |

1. Prepare the Notepad for use, and open the Recorder.

select File, New

click NO to lose the changes

if necessary, size the Notepad window to leave 1" of desktop visible at the bottom of the screen

double-click the Recorder icon

2. Begin recording a macro.

select Macro, Record

3. Name the macro and select [Ctrl][M] as the shortcut keys for future playback.

type MEMO FORM

Press [Tab] to reach the Shortcut Key section

type M

make sure there is an X in the box for the Ctrl key

4. Specify that this macro can be played back in other applications besides Notepad.

   in the Playback section, click the down arrow next to "Same Application"

   select Any Application

5. Tell the recorder to ignore movements of the mouse.

   click the down arrow next to "Clicks + Drags"

   select Ignore Mouse

6. Begin recording.

   click Start

7. In the Notepad document, carefully type the following block of text, entering twice between lines. (If you make mistakes, they will be recorded as well.)

   MEMORANDUM

   TO:

   FROM: (Type your name here)

   DATE:

   RE:

8. Finish recording.

   click the flashing Recorder icon at the bottom of the desktop

   click the OK button in the dialogue box

Activity 4.17   **Playing Back a Longer Macro**

1. Clear the screen in Notepad.

   select File, New

   click NO to lose the changes

2. Play the MEMO FORM macro.

   press [Ctrl][M]

3. Fill in the TO:, DATE: and RE: sections, and type a short memo.

Saving a Set of Macros

1. Switch to the Recorder window.

   press [Alt][Tab] until the Recorder is active

2. Save the set of macros to a file.

   select File, Save

3. Select the A: drive and name the file MYMACS.

   click the down arrow for the list of Drives
   click the A: drive
   click in the File Name box
   type **MYMACS**
   click OK

On Your Own

1. Close the Recorder and try to play the signature macro in the Notepad program. Does it work?

2. Reopen the Recorder and retrieve your MYMACS file.

3. Try playing the signature macro now.

Quick Check

1.   Answer the following questions, true or false.

_____   The Write program is a word processing program.
_____   With Write, you can change fonts and sizes of text.
_____   Character Map is a part of the Write program.
_____   Write documents cannot include graphics.

2.   To print a document in Write, you select

_____.

3.   What is the purpose of the Character Map?

4.   List several of the tools available in Paintbrush.

5.   Describe the procedure for drawing in Paintbrush.

6.   What is the purpose of the Macro Recorder?

Chapter

5

The File Manager

Overview

The File Manager is one of two major components of Windows. You've worked with the other component, the Program Manager, which lets you manage the various application programs used for your day-to-day work, such as the Calculator or Calendar.

The File Manager lets you organize the documents, or files, that are stored on your disks. These files might include letters you created with the Write program or address lists you created with the Cardfile. File Manager gives you a graphical way to look at the storage structure on your disks and to copy and move files from one disk to another.

Unlike the Accessories you've used previously, the File Manager is started from the Main group. In this chapter, you'll use the File Manager to look at directory and file information and to work with your files.

Objectives

- Look at the directory structure on a diskette or hard disk

- Look at the files within a directory

- Move, copy, rename or delete a file

- Create a directory

- Format a new disk for use

- Sort applications with specific documents in one step

The File Manager

You might think of your diskette or hard disk as a file cabinet. The disk is divided into directories which are like file drawers in the cabinet, and the directories hold files which are like file folders in the drawers. The purpose of the File Manager is to let you look, first at the directory arrangement on your disk and then at the individual files within directories.

Activity 5.1

Starting the File Manager

1.   Run the File Manager from the Main group.

double-click the Main program group icon

double-click the File Manager icon

The File Manager window is about the same size as the Program Manager window. Like Program Manager, there are subwindows within it.

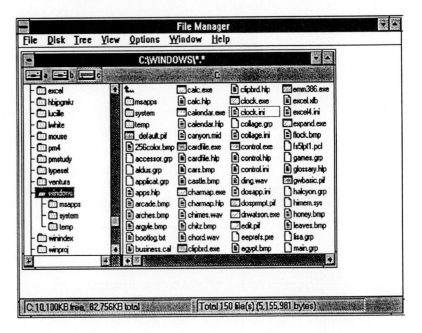

2.   Maximize the File Manager.

click the Maximize button in the upper right corner of the File Manager window

3.   Restore the File Manager to intermediate size.

click the Restore button in the upper right corner of the File Manager window

4. Maximize the subwindow that shows the contents of the current directory.

    click the Maximize button on the subwindow (the subwindow is probably titled "C:\WINDOWS*.")*

    You'll see that the File Manager window is now divided into three main areas: a bar across the top with icons representing the available disk drives, a window on the left with small "folder" icons representing the various directories on the disk, and a window on the right showing the individual documents in the currently selected directory.

5. View the contents of your student disk.

    click the icon for the A: drive

6. View the list of files on the right-hand side.

    if necessary, click the scroll bar on the right

    Notice that there are several kinds of icons representing the different types of files.

7. View the contents of a subdirectory of the A: drive.

    in the window on the left, click the folder icon next to the wakeup directory

8. Return to the main directory on the A: drive.

    in the window on the left, click the folder icon next to the A:\ directory

9. Close the File Manager.

    double-click the File Manager's Control-menu box

    Like the Program Manager, you must click OK to terminate the program.

Activity 5.2

Getting Information from the File Manager

1. Start the File Manager and show all the directories and subdirectories on the A: drive.

double-click the File Manager icon

choose Tree, Expand All

2. Find out what files are in the A:\memos\jones section.

    click jones

3. View only the main directory in the "family tree."

    click the file folder next to A:

    choose Tree, Collapse Branch

4. Get more information about the files in the main directory.

    choose View, All File Details

    Now you can also see the file size and the date and time when the file was last modified. In addition, you'll see the letter "a" to the right of any file that hasn't been backed up since the last time it was worked on.

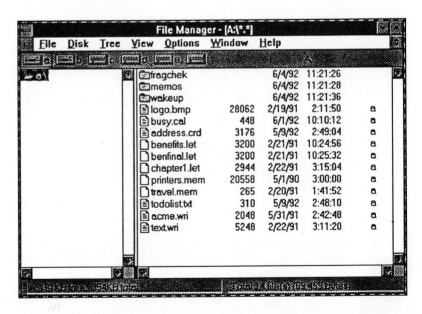

5. Organize the files according to their size.

    choose View, Sort by Size

6. Return to an alphabetical listing.

choose View, Sort by Name

On Your Own

1. Open the File Manager and make sure the directory tree is not maximized.

2. Select Window, New Window.

3. In the new window, click a different disk. You should now have two windows with directory trees.

4. Use Window, Tile to divide the File Manager screen in half and view both disks equally.

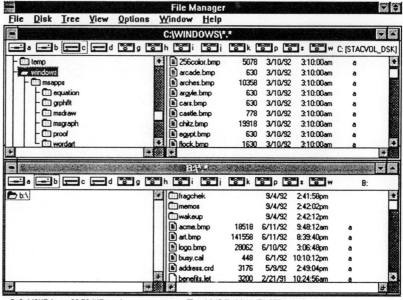

5. Use Window, Cascade to view one disk more prominently than the other.

6. Close the front window.

Managing Files and Directories

As is often the case when working with Windows, there are several ways to copy a file, several ways to move it to a new location — even several ways to delete it. These procedures can be done graphically by manipulating the icons next to the file names. They can also be done with the pull-down menus.

Activity 5.3

Finding and Copying Files

Suppose you wish to copy a file from your hard disk to a floppy disk. This is a good habit to practice — hard disks can have problems, and if you haven't made copies of important data, you could lose many hours of work.

1. Return to the C: drive.

click the icon for the C: drive (or the D: drive if that's where your Windows program is located)

click the icon for C:

2. Find the file called README.WRI.

select File, Search

*type **README.WRI***

click OK

This procedure searches the entire hard drive for a file with the specified name. It may take a little time.

3. If there's more than one file, select the one in the \\windows directory.

click the README.WRI file

4. Copy the file to the A: drive.

while holding down the [Ctrl] key, drag the document icon to the icon for the A: drive

click Yes to confirm the copy

5. Check the A: drive to make sure it got there.

click the icon for the A: drive

The README.WRI file should appear in the list of files on the right.

On Your Own

1. Highlight the README.WRI file on the A: drive.
2. Use the File menu's Rename command. *File, rename*
3. Give the file the new name of READTHIS.NEW.
4. Return to the C:\windows directory.
5. Holding down the [Ctrl] key, select several files that have a size of less than 2000 bytes.
6. Use the File menu to copy the selected files to the A: drive.

Deleting Files

Caution: Once a file has been deleted, the File Manager cannot recover it! Don't delete a file until you've made a copy somewhere else, or until you're sure you won't need it again.

Activity 5.4

Deleting a File

You should have a window open displaying the files on the A: drive.

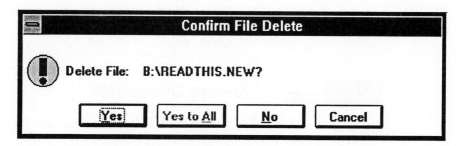

1. Delete the READTHIS.NEW file on the A: drive.

    click READTHIS.NEW

    select File, Delete

click the OK button in the Delete dialog box

click the Yes button to confirm

2.   Is the file removed from the list?

Activity 5.5 | Preparing a Disk for Use

1.   Place a new, blank, double-sided, double-density disk in the A: drive.

   remove the student disk

   insert the new, blank disk

2.   Format the disk to prepare it for use.

   select Disk, Format Disk

3.   Specify the location and capacity of the disk.

   select Drive A:

   select the lower number in the capacity box (either 360K or 720K)

4.   Format the disk.

   click OK

   click Yes

   The disk will be prepared for future use.

5.   When finished, don't format another disk.

   click No

Activity 5.6 | Creating Directories

1.   Select the newly formatted disk in the A: drive.

   click the icon for the A: drive

2.   Divide the disk into three directories for the different kinds of projects it will contain.

select File, Create Directory

type REPORTS and press [Enter]

select File, Create Directory

type ORDERS and press [Enter]

select File, Create Directory

type LETTERS and press [Enter]

Notice the icons for each new directory.

Working with Files

You've probably noticed that there are several kinds of icons which represent different kinds of files. When you work with the File Manager, these icons give you important information about the types of documents on your disk.

The three main types of files are defined below.

File Type	Icon	Explanation
Associated Document ⚡	📄	A document used with a program that Windows recognizes.
Unassociated Document ⚡	📄	A document that Windows does not recognize.
Program	▨	A file that gives the computer instructions to run a program.

Activity 5.7

Using Files to Start Programs

1. Select the C: drive.

   click the icon for the C: drive

2. Start the Calculator program from the \windows directory.

click the \windows directory

double-click the CALC.EXE file in the right-hand window

3. Close the Calculator.

double-click the Calculator's Control-menu box

4. Use the File Menu to start the Cardfile program.

select File, Run

*type **CARDFILE.EXE** and press [Enter]*

5. Close the Cardfile.

double-click the Cardfile's Control-menu box

6. Return to the A: drive.

click the icon for the A: drive

if necessary, click the icon next to A:

7. Start the Cardfile program with your list of addresses.

double-click the associated file icon next to the ADDRESS.CRD file

8. Close the Cardfile.

select File, Exit

9. See if you can start a program with the TRAVEL.MEM document.

double-click the unassociated file icon next to the TRAVEL.MEM file

click OK in the message box

You can't start a program with this file because the file hasn't been associated with a program. Windows doesn't know which program created the file, and so can't start a program or open the file. In the next activity, you'll see how to associate files.

Activity 5.8

Associating Files

1. Associate files that have an extension of .MEM to the Notepad program.

   click TRAVEL.MEM

   select File, Associate

   select Text File (notepad.exe) from the drop-down list

   click OK

   Notice that the icon for TRAVEL.MEM has changed.

2. Start the Notepad program with the TRAVEL.MEM document.

   double-click TRAVEL.MEM

3. Close the Notepad.

   select File, Exit

4. Try starting the Notepad with another one of the .MEM files.

   double-click PRINTERS.MEM

On Your Own

1. Associate files that have the extension .LET with the Write program.

2. Start the Write program by double-clicking one of the .LET files.

3. Remove the association of .LET files so that they don't automatically start any program.

Quick Check

1. How can you see all the directories and subdirectories on a disk?

2. What command shows file sizes, dates, and times?

3. Describe how to move a file from one directory to another.

4. Describe how to copy a file.

5. How do you format a diskette from the File Manager?

6. What is the purpose of associating a file? How do you do it?

Chapter

6

The Control Panel

Now that you know the mechanics of the Windows interface, you can begin to customize the appearance of the screen and the way you want to use Windows. You can change the colors and patterns on your screen, as well as the way the mouse and keyboard work. In this chapter, you'll explore the possibilities provided by the Control Panel program.

Objectives

- Change the time and date

- Adjust the mouse's speed of operation

- Customize the Windows screen colors

- Change the Windows desktop

- Protect the screen from "burn-in" with a screen saver

The Control Panel

The Control Panel is in the Main program group. The Control Panel gives you the ability to work with the features of Windows that are integral to all programs. When you make a change with the Control Panel, the results affect all your Windows programs.

For example, every program uses the mouse. If you have trouble controlling the mouse, you might prefer that the mouse pointer move more slowly. You'd want the slower speed to apply in all your Windows programs.

If this is the case, you can change the speed with which the mouse moves or "tracks" across the screen. The new speed would apply in Write, Paintbrush, and all your other Windows programs.

The table on the following page describes the various subprograms in the Control Panel.

The Control Panel

Icon	Program Purpose	Where Described
	Change screen colors	Chapter 6
Fonts	View available fonts, or typestyles	Chapter 7
Ports	Change the rate at which devices like modems communicate	Refer to your Microsoft Windows User's Guide
Mouse	Control the speed of mouse movement and clicking	Chapter 6
Desktop	Change patterns, wallpaper, icon spacing, and screen savers	Chapter 6
Keyboard	Control the key repeat rate	Refer to your Microsoft Windows User's Guide
Printers	Configure and set up printers and printer ports	Chapter 7
International	Change settings to match specifications for other countries	Chapter 6
Date/Time	Set the computer's internal clock	Chapter 6
386 Enhanced	Control memory and virtual memory management	Refer to your Microsoft Windows User's Guide
Drivers	Configure drivers for add-on devices such as sound cards	Refer to your Microsoft Windows User's Guide
Sound	Control the use of an installed sound card	Refer to your Microsoft Windows User's Guide

Activity 6.1 | ## Changing Mouse Speed

1. Open the Control Panel in the Main program group.

   double-click the Main program group icon

   double-click the Control Panel icon

2. View the new group of icons representing Control Panel subprograms.

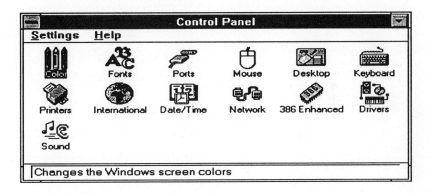

3. Open the Mouse subprogram.

   double-click the Mouse icon

4. Adjust the tracking speed.

   click the left end of the scroll bar below "Slow" in the Mouse Tracking Speed area

   move the mouse around on the screen

   Do you notice that it moves more slowly?

5. Speed up the tracking.

   click twice on the right end of the scroll bar below "Fast."

   move the mouse around on the screen

   Is it faster?

6.   Pick a speed that suits you.

use the scroll bar arrows to pick your optimal speed

click OK

Activity 6.2	## Changing Double-Click Speed

1.   Reopen the Mouse program and slow the double-click speed.

double-click the Mouse icon

click the left side of the scroll bar in the Double Click Speed area

2.   Test the new speed.

double-click in the Test box

If the box changes color, you have successfully double-clicked. If it remains the same color, you need to double-click at a different speed.

3.   Increase the double-click speed and test the new speed.

click the right side of the scroll bar in the Double Click Speed area

double-click in the Test box

4.   Pick a speed that's right for you.

use the scroll bar to select your optimal double-click speed

click OK

Activity 6.3	## Changing the Date and Time

1.   From the Control Panel run the Date/Time subprogram.

double-click Date/Time

press the [Tab] key several times while watching

the Date & Time dialog box

What happens?

2. If the date and time are incorrect, use the up/down arrow buttons to change them, then exit the program.

    click the up or down arrow for date or time

    click OK

Changing Colors

You can also customize the appearance of your Windows screen from the Control Panel. You may choose from a number of preselected color schemes, or you may create and name your own color scheme. You may even create your own custom colors.

Activity 6.4

Changing Windows Colors

1. With the Control Panel open, select a new color.

    double-click the Color icon

    click the down arrow on the Color Schemes list box

    click the down scroll bar arrow until the Pastel scheme is visible

    select the Pastel color scheme from the list

    Notice how the color scheme has changed in the example below the list.

2. Try some other color schemes.

    click the down arrow on the Color Schemes list box

    scroll through the list

    select a color scheme from the list

3. With the Ocean color scheme as an example, open the Color Palette.

click the down arrow on the Color Schemes list box

select Ocean

click Color Palette

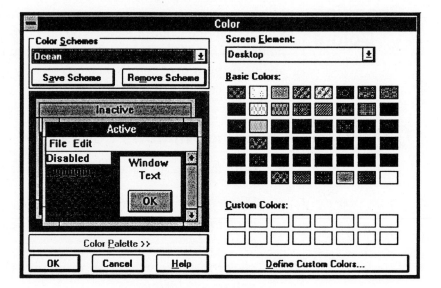

4. View the list of window component names and change the color of one.

click the down arrow in the Screen Element list box

select Active Title Bar

select a color from the Basic Colors palette

click OK

On Your Own

1. Design your own color scheme using the color palette.

2. Save the color scheme with the name LOVELY.

3. Select Define Custom Colors.

4. See if you can design a custom color and add it to the Lovely color scheme.

The Windows Desktop

If you like, you can do even more redecorating with Windows. Using the Desktop subprogram of the Control Panel, you can choose patterns and/or wallpaper for your desktop, as well as screen savers to protect your screen.

Activity 6.5

Changing the Desktop

1. With the Control Panel open, minimize any other programs running.

   click the Minimize button on any other visible applications

   The Control Panel should now be the only open window on your Desktop.

2. Open the Desktop program.

   double-click the Desktop icon

3. Change the Desktop Pattern.

   select Edit Pattern

   click the down arrow on the Pattern drop-down list box

   select the Critters pattern from the list

   Notice the pattern in the Sample box.

4. View the change on your screen.

   click OK until you are back at the Control Panel

   Notice the new desktop you have selected.

On Your Own

1. Run the Desktop subprogram and select a Wallpaper.

2. Experiment with the difference between Center and Tile options.

3. Experiment with the Cursor Blink Rate.

Activity 6.6

Screen Savers

1. With the Control Panel open, select the Desktop.

   double-click the Desktop icon

2. View the various Screen Saver names.

   click the down arrow next to the list of Screen Saver Names

3. Test a Screen Saver.

   select Flying Windows

   click the Test button

4. When finished observing the patterns, return to the active screen.

   move the mouse or press a key on the keyboard

5. Select a Screen Saver and set it to go off after one minute of inactivity.

   select a Screen Saver from the list

   use the down arrow key next to "Minutes" to set the Delay to 1

   click OK

6. Test the delay.

   do not touch the mouse or keyboard for one full minute

   The Screen Saver should go into effect after one minute.

| Activity 6.7 | **International Settings** |

Many countries use a 24-hour clock and a different procedure for typing dates. In addition, most foreign alphabets include characters that are not on the standard keyboard of an American computer. Windows lets you change these settings with the International option of the Control Panel.

1.   With the Main window open, start the File Manager.

double-click the File Manager icon

select View, All File Details

Notice that the save times of the files are all in a 12-hour format. There is no unambiguous way to know if files were saved in the morning or the evening.

2.   Minimize the File Manager.

click the Minimize button on the File Manager window

3.   With the Control Panel open, start the International program.

double-click International

4. Change the Time Format to a 24-hour standard.

    click Change in the Time Format area

    click the 24-hour radio button

    click OK

    click OK in the International dialog box

5. Return to the File Manager.

    use [Alt][Tab] to return to the File Manager

    The times at which the files were saved should now be in 24-hour format.

On Your Own

1. Use the International option of the Control Panel to change the date format.

2. Turn on the Century feature to show dates as "1992" instead of "92."

3. Return to the File Manager to view the new date formats on the files.

4. Return the Date format to two digits for years.

5. Return the Time format to 12 hours.

Windows Initialization Files

Many of the settings you change through the Control Panel are contained in the Windows initialization files. You should know a little about the format of these files, what settings are in each, and how to make changes to them.

Windows automatically chooses an operating mode each time you begin. This happens because Windows has information about your configuration and settings stored in *initialization files*. Each time Windows begins, it reads the initialization files to determine how it should start and run.

There are two main initialization files that Windows uses: WIN.INI and SYSTEM.INI. In addition to these two, several of the applications that are supplied with Windows have their own initialization files; for example, Program Manager (PROGMAN.INI) and Control Panel (CONTROL.INI). Other Windows applications, like Excel or PageMaker, may create and maintain their own initialization files as well.

INI File Format

Though they contain information about different aspects of your environment, initialization files have a common format.

- They are *ASCII text files*; that is, they contain only alphanumeric characters and no special control codes.

- They are divided into sections, each of which begins with a header that labels the section. The section header is shown in square brackets, as in: [ports] or [fonts].

- After the header, there is a list of keywords and assignments which define the settings for that section.

- Each keyword is followed by an equals sign (=) and a value, like: MouseSpeed=1.

You can find detailed descriptions of each section and setting in the .WRI files that are included in your Windows directory. For WIN.INI this is WININI.WRI; and for SYSTEM.INI, it is SYSINI.WRI.

Activity 6.8

Reading the Text Files

You can use Write to read and print the text files that explain WIN.INI and SYSTEM.INI files.

1. Start Write from the Accessories group.

double-click the Write icon

2. Open the text file for WIN.INI.

select File, Open

double-click WININI.WRI

3. Maximize Write.

click the maximize button

4. Review the information.

click the scroll arrows to scroll within the file

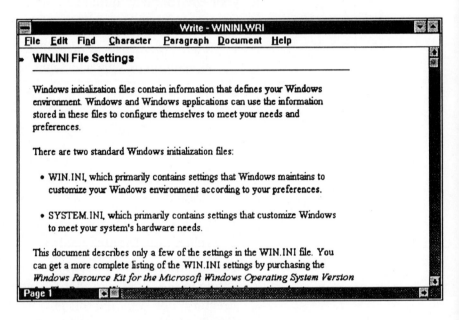

The WIN.INI File

Windows creates the WIN.INI file when you install it. All of the settings in WIN.INI are set to the default values defined by Windows. You can change the settings as you like to suit your preferences.

The WIN.INI file contains information about your preferences for the Windows environment. You can change settings in the file in two ways: through the Control Panel or by editing it directly using an ASCII text editor.

WIN.INI is divided into sections. Which sections you have depends on your hardware and software. Other Windows applications that you load may also add sections to the WIN.INI file.

The SYSTEM.INI File

The SYSTEM.INI file contains settings that describe your hardware configuration. The file contains global system information that Windows uses when it starts. You can customize SYSTEM.INI to meet your hardware requirements.

In general, you cannot change SYSTEM.INI settings from the Control Panel. You can change some of the settings through the Windows Setup program, or you can edit the file directly to make changes.

Caution: Changing settings in either WIN.INI or SYSTEM.INI should be done very carefully. Incorrect settings in SYSTEM.INI can completely disable your system, while undesirable results in Windows operation can occur if you change WIN.INI. Before modifying either file, **be sure to make a backup copy** so that you can recover if there is a problem.

Activity 6.9

Backing Up WIN.INI

To prepare for making changes to the WIN.INI file, you will first make a copy of the file.

1.   Start the File Manager from the Main Group.

     double-click the File Manager icon

2.   Scroll if necessary to see the Windows subdirectory and select it.

     double-click the Window subdirectory

3.   Find the WIN.INI file and select it.

     click the WIN.INI file

4.   Copy WIN.INI to a new file on a floppy diskette.

     select File, Copy

     *in the To box, type **OLDWIN.INI***

     click Copy

You now have a copy of WIN.INI in case something should go wrong while you are editing or if you just want to set things up as they were before.

Using Sysedit

You can edit the INI files using the Notepad, any other ASCII text editor, or a word processor that can save files in ASCII format. As an alternative, you can use a utility supplied with Windows called Sysedit.

Sysedit is a System Configuration Editor. In addition to allowing you to see and make changes to both INI files at once, Sysedit also opens windows for your CONFIG.SYS and AUTOEXEC.BAT files. You can start Sysedit by using the File, Run command from the Program Manager menu.

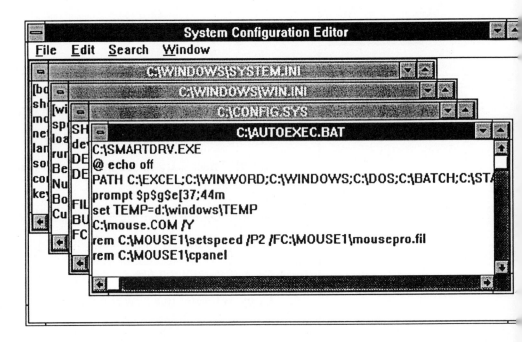

| **Activity 6.10** | **Viewing INI Files with Sysedit** |

1. Start the Sysedit utility from the Program Manager.

   select File, Run

   *type **SYSEDIT** and press [Enter]*

   The Sysedit window opens with the two INI files and two DOS startup files displayed in cascaded windows.

2. Bring the WIN.INI file to the top.

   click in the WIN.INI file window

3. Maximize the window and examine the file.

   click the maximize button

   click the scroll arrows to scroll within the file

   Do you notice some of the settings you changed in the Control Panel?

4. Close Sysedit.

   select File, Exit

Quick Check

1. Explain the purpose of the Control Panel.

2. List at least four of the Control Panel's subprograms.

3. What settings can you control with the Mouse subprogram?

4. Which Control Panel program would you use to add wallpaper? To use a screen saver?

5. What is the purpose of the initialization (INI) files?

6. List the two main INI files.

7. What utility can you use to edit the INI files?

Chapter
7

Fonts and Printing

Overview

Windows 3.1 incorporates a technology called TrueType fonts to become a real WYSIWYG [What You See is What You Get] environment. TrueType was developed for the Macintosh® by Apple® and then licensed by Microsoft. With TrueType fonts, characters look the same on screen as they do when printed, regardless of the type of monitor or printer you're using.

Before you can use a printer in Windows, you must install and configure it, and then set it up. When you go through Windows Setup, as described in the previous chapter, you can select and install printers for operation with Windows. You probably installed at least one printer when you installed Windows. However, you may need to change the printer selection or add another printer. Besides adding printers, you may want to add fonts to the setup of your selected printer.

In this chapter, you'll learn about TrueType fonts and how to install, configure, and set up a printer. You'll also see how to print from Windows and how to control printing using the Print Manager.

Objectives

- Understand screen and printer fonts

- Select and configure a printer

- Print from Windows

- Use Print Manager to control printing

About Fonts

The term *font* refers to a subset of a typeface. A typeface (e.g., Courier or Times Roman) consists of letter designs. Typefaces and their names are usually copyrighted.

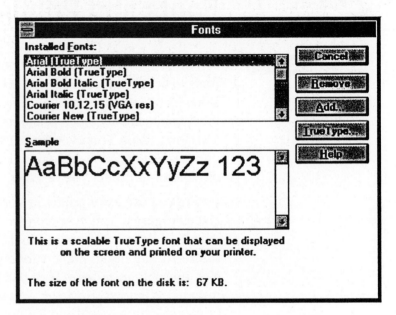

A font describes a subset of a typeface with certain attributes. A given typeface may have four separate fonts:

- Normal

- **Bold**

- *Italic*

- ***Bold Italic***

Helvetica, for example, is a typeface; but Helvetica Bold is a font, as is Helvetica Italic.

Typefaces and fonts can be spaced in one of two ways:

Fixed-space — In fixed-space fonts, every character in the set takes up the same amount of horizontal space.

Proportional — In proportional fonts, the horizontal spacing changes with character width.

As an example, in a proportional font, w takes more horizontal space than i. Some printers only support fixed-space fonts.

Screen Fonts

Fonts that are used for characters on your display are known as *screen fonts*. Windows comes with several screen fonts. Windows screen fonts are of three types: raster fonts, vector fonts, and outline fonts.

Raster Fonts

Raster fonts are bitmaps of letter designs. Raster fonts come in specific sizes to go with different display resolutions.

Raster fonts can be scaled, but only in even multiples of the sizes in which they are supplied. In terms of appearance, raster fonts that are scaled too far from their original size can look jagged.

Raster fonts supplied with Windows 3.1 are: MS Serif (formerly known as Tms Rmn in Windows 3.0), MS Sans Serif (Helv in Windows 3.0), Courier, and System.

Vector Fonts

Vector fonts are stored as mathematical models; they are letter designs defined as lines drawn between points.

Like raster fonts, vector fonts can be scaled, but with an important difference. Vector fonts can be scaled to any size. For this reason, vector fonts generally look better than raster fonts in larger sizes.

Vector fonts supplied with Windows 3.1 are: Terminal, Roman, Modern, and Script.

Outline Fonts (TrueType)

TrueType fonts are a new implementation of outline fonts that are scalable. The main advantages in using TrueType fonts are that they look the same on your display screen as they do on your printer and that they are smooth-looking at any size.

Thirteen TrueType fonts are included with Windows 3.1: Courier, Times Roman, and Helvetica in bold, italic, and bold italic versions, and a symbol font called Wingdings. The names Helvetica and Times Roman have not been licensed by Microsoft, and so are called Arial and Times New Roman.

Printer Fonts

A *printer font* is a font description used by the printer to produce a font. Besides printable screen fonts, printer fonts are of two main types: device fonts or downloadable fonts.

Device (or Hardware) Fonts These fonts are part of the printer hardware. They can be built-in to the printer or can be supplied on a cartridge or card.

Downloadable (Software) Fonts These fonts exist on your hard drive and are sent to the printer when needed.

Some printers, for example, dot matrix ones, support only device fonts. Printers that support the Hewlett-Packard Printer Control Language (HPPCL) can support font cartridges, downloadable fonts, and vector screen fonts.

Device Fonts

When you set up your printer, a list of available font cartridges for the printer, along with the maximum number of cartridges that can be used, is shown in the Printer Setup dialog box.

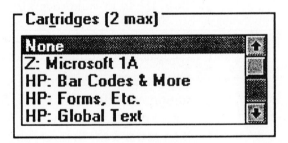

This is how you tell Windows which font cartridges to use. If you always use the same cartridge, you need only set this once.

Software Fonts

Laser-Jet compatible software fonts are available from a variety of vendors. How you install the software fonts depends on the source. You install Hewlett-Packard soft fonts using the PCL Font Installer. Soft fonts supplied by other vendors are installed with their own installation program.

Selecting a Printer

Before you can use a printer with Windows you must install it, configure it, and set it up.

Installation means making a file of information about your printer (called a *printer driver*) available to Windows. This was probably done when the Windows program was installed on your computer, but you might have occasion to change that selection or add an additional printer to the list of those available.

Configuring a printer means connecting your printer driver to the proper computer port or connector. This will ensure that information goes to the same connector to which the printer is attached.

Setting up a printer means selecting options for your particular use of the printer. For example choosing 8.5" by 11" or 8.5" by 14" inch paper, printing in portrait or landscape, or, selecting letter quality or draft mode.

Of the three processes, setting up is the one with which you will be most concerned because it's the one you'll use most often. In the next activity, you won't install or configure a printer, but you'll see how it's done.

Activity 7.1

Installing a Printer

1. Run the Printers subprogram in the Control Panel.

    double-click the Printers icon

The printer installed for your computer is listed in the Installed Printers box and is listed as the default printer.

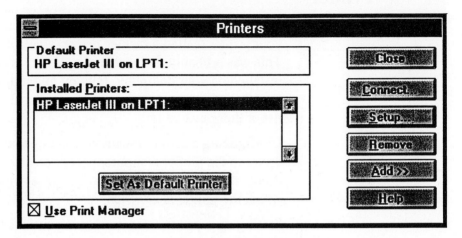

2. The chevrons (>>) following Add on the Add button mean that it is an intermediate dialog box (there is still another level below).

    click the Add>> button

3. Scroll through the list in the List of Printers box to find the HP LaserJet Series II.

    scroll the printer list

    The printer list parallels the printer drivers found on the original Windows diskettes. To install a new printer, you must have those diskettes available. Had you wished to install the new printer, you would have selected the Install button.

Configuring a Printer

After you've installed a printer, you must configure it and make it active before you can use it. Standard PC systems can have up to three *parallel* printer ports which are known as **LPT** ports and up to four *serial* printer ports, which are known as **COM** ports.

When you configure a printer, you're assigning the printer to one of these ports. You can have an *active* printer for each port in the system. You can install more printers, but only one can be active on each port at a time.

To begin, you select the printer and click the Connect button in the Printers dialog. You will see the Connect dialog box. In this dialog box, you assign the printer to a port and set some options for the printer.

Note: In addition to the standard ports, you'll also see a File: choice. This choice allows you to assign output to a file. Each time you print with this printer selected, Windows will ask for an output file name.

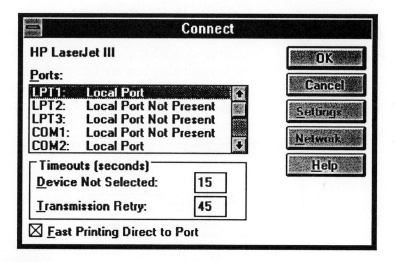

Activity 7.2 | Configuring a Printer

1. Go to the Connect dialog box.

click the Connect button

The usual choice for a printer port is LPT1. You might change that if you have more than one printer.

Device not Selected tells Windows how long to wait before letting you know that it is unable to print to the printer.

Transmission Retry sets the length of time Windows waits before retrying if the printer signals that it is busy.

2. Make no changes to the Connect dialog box.

click Cancel

Setting Up a Printer

Because printers differ, Printer Setup dialog boxes differ as well. The box shown on this page is for the *HP LaserJet Series III*.

Activity 7.3

Setting Up a Printer

1. Go to the Setup dialog box.

click the Setup button

Look at the Printer Setup dialog box. Note the drop-down list choices. While some of the selections in the dialog box are self-explanatory, you can get help for any that you don't understand by selecting Help.

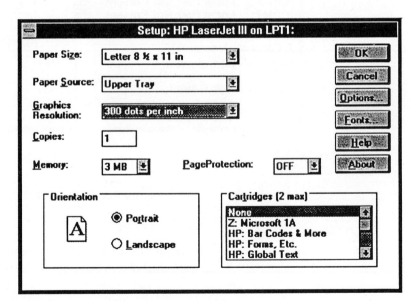

2. Return to Control Panel.

select the Cancel button in each dialog box until at the Control Panel

You'll find a Print Setup command in the File menu of many Windows applications where the printer is to be used. When you select that command, you may use the Setup dialog box to control the manner in which the application will use the printer.

Printing from Windows

Once you've completed the printer setup process, printing from Windows is quite simple. The printer and settings you've selected are available to all Windows applications. You do not have to redefine the printer for each individual application.

Also, unlike most DOS applications, Windows allows you to perform other tasks while printing. When you print from a Windows application, printing takes place in the background and other tasks can proceed in the foreground. This is accomplished through a *print spooler* known as the Print Manager.

The Print Manager

The Print Manager is a program in the Main program group. Although the Print Manager is by default enabled for your printer, it's relatively transparent to you, unless there's a printing problem.

When you choose the Print command from a Windows application, the application sends a print request to the Print Manager. The Print Manager logs in the request and places the print job in a queue. It then directs the job to the printer.

All of this happens in the background. The data from the application is actually sent to a temporary file which the Print Manager schedules for printing. Once the application has sent the information, you can continue to work on other tasks.

The Print Manager icon appears on the desktop when you start a print job. If printing is successful, the Print Manager deletes the temporary file and closes automatically.

If the Print Manager is inactive, you can start it by double-clicking its icon in the Main program group. The Print Manager window opens, but no print jobs are in the queue.

While the Print Manager is active, double-clicking its icon on the desktop will show you the print queue and the status of your print jobs.

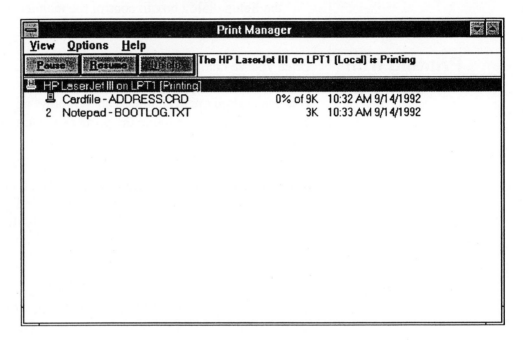

All pending print jobs are shown in the queue. The first line shows the destination printer, its port, and its status. Status is shown in brackets. The most common are: [Printing], [Stalled], and [Idle]. If you have more than one printer, the print queue will include a section for each.

Beneath the printer line are the print jobs, listed in the order in which they were sent to print. For each print job, you'll see the name of the application that made the print request, the name of the file to be printed, the size of the file, and the date and time the request was made.

When Problems Occur

If your printer isn't ready (e.g., it's not on-line, it's out of paper, or it has a paper jam), the Print Manager cannot successfully complete a print request. In this situation, you may receive an alert box like this:

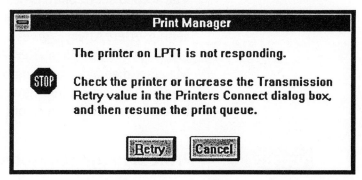

You must click OK to dismiss the box. You can then correct the printer problem. After you've done so, the Print Manager will automatically resume the queue.

Print Manager Options

The Print Manager Options menu commands allow you to control how the Print Manager schedules print requests and what it does when there's a problem.

The first three choices have to do with scheduling priority. You can have print requests processed as Low Priority, Medium Priority, or High Priority. The priority with which requests are processed is relative to other tasks in the system.

Priority	Printing	Foreground Tasks
Low	Slower	Faster
High	Faster	Slower

With Medium Priority, the system allows about the same amount of time to the Print Manager as it does to foreground applications.

You can choose the setting that best meets your needs, and you only need to set it once. However, if you want to change it for a particular session or print job, you can.

The second set of options deals with how the Print Manager responds when it encounters a problem. The first setting, Alert Always, gives you immediate warning of a printer problem. When Alert Always is selected, the Print Manager displays a warning box as soon as an error occurs. The last setting, Ignore if Inactive, will give no indication at all that an error has occurred.

Activity 7.4   Print Manager Options

To change the way Windows handles print requests, change the options in the Print Manager.

1. Select Print Manager from the Main Group.

    double-click the Print Manager icon

    The Print Manager window opens with no jobs in the print queue.

2. Select the Options menu and examine the choices.

    select Options

3. What priority results in the fastest printing?

4. What's the effect of Alert Always?

5. Minimize the Print Manager.

    click the Minimize button

Drag and Drop Printing

If you have the Print Manager running, you can use a feature called Drag and Drop to print Windows files. This procedure only works with Windows applications and with files that have been associated with the appropriate application.

With the Print Manager running as an icon on the desktop, start the File Manager. Locate the associated file you want to print. Drag the file icon from the File Manager and drop it on the Print Manager.

Windows starts the application that created the file, opens the file, and presents the Print dialog box for the application. Make any changes you require, then click OK, and your document will be printed.

Activity 7.5 | Printing with Drag and Drop

1. Start the File Manager from the Main Group.

    double-click the File Manager icon

    The File Manager window opens with the last directory window you viewed open.

2. If necessary, select the A: drive and locate the file ACME.WRI.

    click the A: icon

    click the A:\ icon

    Do you see the ACME.WRI file?

3. Print the file.

    drag the ACME.WRI document icon to the Print Manager icon and drop it

    in the dialog box, click OK

    The file will be printed.

Printing from Non-Windows Applications

Because most non-Windows applications are not written for a multitasking environment, they are not able to share system resources like a printer in the way that Windows applications do. Non-Windows applications do not use the Print Manager, and must print directly to the printer.

If you try to print from Windows and a non-Windows application at the same time, you may get a Device Conflict message box. In this case, you must assign the printer either to Windows or to the non-Windows application.

If you select Windows, the non-Windows application will get a printer error, and the Print Manager will continue printing Windows requests. If you select the non-Windows application, the Print Manager will suspend Windows print requests until the application is finished printing. It will then resume Windows printing.

Quick Check

1.   What is the difference between a font and a typeface?

2.   TrueType fonts are _____ fonts that are _____.

3.   List the three steps for selecting a printer.

4.   What program do you use to install and configure a printer?

5.   What does the Print Manager do?

6.   Describe the procedure for drag and drop printing.

Chapter

8

Program Manager

You've seen the Program Manager as you worked with items from both the Main and Accessories groups. You may want to learn more about what the Program Manager does and how you can control it. In this chapter, you'll learn about program groups and icons and about Program Manager options. You'll also see how to create and delete program groups and items and how to work with the StartUp group.

- Understand program groups and program items

- Arrange the Program Manager display

- Use Program Manager options

- Create a program group

- Add items to a program group

- Delete program items and groups

- Use the StartUp group

About Program Manager

The Program Manager is the central application in Windows. When you start Windows, you start the Program Manager. Thereafter, the Program Manager runs, either in a window or in the background, until you exit Windows.

Program Groups and Items

The Program Manager window contains program groups which, in turn, contain program items that start programs. The Program Manager menu bar affects these groups and items.

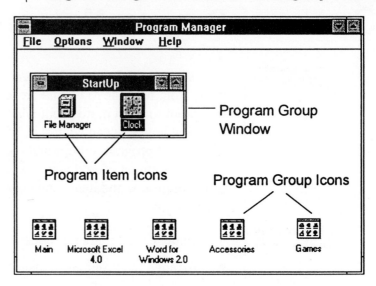

- Program groups appear in Program Manager as group windows or group icons.

- Neither group windows nor group icons can be dragged outside the borders of the Program Manager window.

- Windows comes with predefined program groups that include: Main, Accessories, StartUp, Applications, and Games.

   Note: If Windows was installed with the Custom Setup option, you may not have an Applications group. If you do not have an Applications group, or if you want to add an application to the group, you can use Windows Setup to add the icon. See Appendix B for more information.

Arranging Windows and Icons

You can control the way that program groups are displayed in the Program Manager through the **Window menu** commands.

- The **Tile** command arranges program group windows side-by-side in the Program Manager window.

- The **Cascade** command arranges program group windows in an overlapping fashion one on top of another.

- The **Arrange Icons** command arranges program group icons in a row at the bottom of the Program Manager window.

Besides these commands, the Window menu includes the name of every program group window. The currently selected window is shown with a check mark next to its name.

Activity 8.1 | Arranging Icons

1. Begin by closing any program groups.

   double-click the Control-menu box for any open groups

2. Move the group icons around in the Program Manager window.

   drag the Accessories group to a new location
   drag the Main group to a new location
   drag the Games group to a new location

3. Rearrange the group icons.

   select Window, Arrange Icons

   The program group icons are arranged in a row.

Activity 8.2 | Arranging Group Windows

1. Begin by maximizing the Program Manager window.

   click the maximize button

2. Open two program groups.

   double-click the Accessories group icon

select Window, Main

3. Arrange the group windows side-by-side.

    select Window, Tile

    The group windows are tiled inside the Program Manager window.

4. Rearrange the group windows.

    select Window, Cascade

On Your Own

1. Open two or three groups and arrange them using either the Tile or Cascade command.

2. What happens when you minimize a group window and then restore it? You should notice that the group window is restored to its previous size and location; i.e., as it was when Tiled or Cascaded.

3. Open several groups and arrange them by sizing and dragging. Use the Window, Arrange Icons command to arrange icons within a program group window.

The Options Menu

You don't have to change the display of program groups and of the Program Manager unless you want a particular arrangement. If you do want to define the display, you can create an arrangement once and save it. The commands that control the display are on the **Options Menu**.

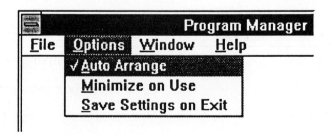

- **The Auto Arrange** command automatically rearranges the program-item icons in a group window whenever the window's size is changed, or items are added or moved.

- The **Minimize on Use** command reduces the Program Manager window to an icon when you start an application that starts in a window.

- The **Save Settings on Exit** command saves the arrangement of Program Manager windows and icons when you quit Windows.

The commands on the Options menu turn on or off the feature they describe. When the feature is in effect, a check mark appears next to the command.

If you want to keep an arrangement of program groups and the Program Manager, you can do so by: arranging the groups as you want them to appear; selecting Options, Save Settings on Exit; and exiting Windows. The next time you start Windows, the arrangement you selected will appear on the screen.

Note: Once you've successfully saved the settings, you may want to turn off the Save Settings option. That way, any changes you make during an individual session will not replace your settings.

Activity 8.3 | Program Manager Options

To begin, you should have the Program Manager with the Main group window open on your screen.

1.   Change the Program Manager options.

select Options, Minimize on Use

This will cause the Program Manager window to be minimized to an icon when you start another application.

2.   Start another application.

double-click the Read Me icon in the Main group

What happened to the Program Manager? It should be minimized on the desktop.

3.   Close the Read Me file and restore Program Manager.

double-click the Control-menu box

double-click the Program Manager icon

On Your Own

1.   Turn on the Save Settings on Exit option, exit Windows, and then restart Windows. Was your arrangement saved?

2.   Turn all options off.

Creating Program Groups

Program groups can help you to organize your screen desktop and work more efficiently. You can create your own groups to organize application and document icons in a way that works for you.

For example, if you're working on a project for which you prepare documents with Write and include graphics from Paint, you might want to put these accessories and the files that you create with them in a group. In that way, you'll be able to easily find them when you need them.

• To begin creating a program group, you should be in the Program Manager window with all other groups closed.

• You use the Program Manager File, New command to create a program group.

- When you create a group, the empty group window will open on the screen.

Once you've created a group, you can add program items to it in several ways. In the following activities, you'll create a group and add items to it.

Activity 8.4

Your Own Program Group

1. Begin by closing program groups.

   double-click the Control-menu box for any open groups

2. Create the group.

   select File, New

   make sure Program Group is selected

   click OK

3. Give the group a name.

   type **DOCUMENTS** *as the Description for the group*

   click OK

   An empty program group with the title Documents appears on your screen.

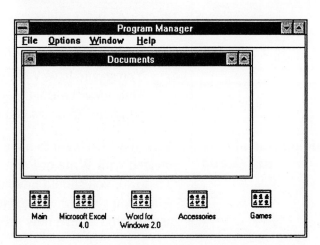

Adding Items to a Group

You'll want to have both Write and Paint available in your new group. To add an item to a group, you must have the group window open. An easy way to add a program item is to copy its icon from another group.

Activity 8.5

Adding Program Items

1. Open the Accessories Group.

   double-click the Accessories group icon

2. Move the Accessories window so you can see Documents.

   click and drag the title bar of the Accessories window

3. Copy the Write icon to the Documents group.

   hold down the [Ctrl] key and drag the Write icon from Accessories to Documents

   Caution: If you don't hold down the [Ctrl] key while dragging, you'll be moving the program item from the Accessories group to the new group.

4. Copy the Paint icon to the Documents group.

   hold down the [Ctrl] key and drag the Paint icon from Accessories to Documents

5. Close the Accessories group.

   double-click the control-menu box

   You should have Write and Paint icons in both groups. This doesn't mean that you have two copies of these programs. It means you can start them from either group.

Adding Documents to a Group

You may also want to have some of the files that you've created with Write or Paint available in your group as well. To do so, you should have the group window open. Then, when you select the File, New command, Windows will assume you want a new program item.

Activity 8.6 | Adding a Document

1. Add the ACME letter to your group.

   select File, New
   make sure Program Item is selected
   choose OK

2. Give the item a name and identify the command line for starting it.

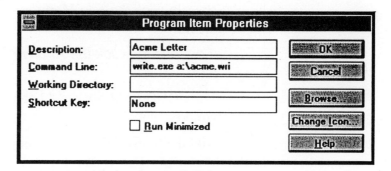

*type **Acme Letter** as the Description*
press [Tab]
*type **WRITE.EXE A:\ACME.WRI***
click OK

The Write icon with the description you typed appears in the group. You can now start to work with the document by double-clicking its icon.

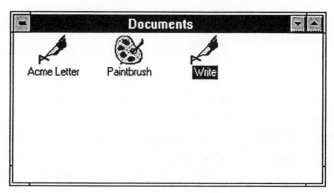

Another Way to Add Items

Another, perhaps easier way to add items to a program group is to drag the file icon from the File Manager and drop it into the program group window or icon. This feature gives you the flexibility of looking around for your document files and of adding multiple items at the same time.

Activity 8.7

Drag and Drop

1. Start the File Manager and locate the LOGO.BMP file.

double-click the File Manager icon in the Main group

if necessary, click the A: drive icon and the A:\ icon

The LOGO.BMP file should appear in the files window.

2. Add the LOGO.BMP file to your group.

move File Manager so you can see it and the Documents group

drag the file icon from File Manager to the Documents group

The Paint icon with the file name for a description appears in the group. You can now start to work with the graphic by double-clicking its icon.

On Your Own

1. Add the TEXT.WRI file to your group.

2. Try starting Write or Paint from one of the document icons.

3. Close the Documents group.

Deleting Items and Groups

If you no longer need an item or a group, you can delete it. You can reduce clutter and have only the most current, useful arrangement on your screen desktop.

To delete a program item: First, select (single click) the item in the program group window. The icon's title bar will be highlighted. Then, choose File, Delete from the Program Manager menu bar. After you confirm your choice in the Caution box, the item is removed from the group.

To delete a program group: First, minimize the group window to an icon. Select (single click) the program group icon. Then, choose File, Delete from the Program Manager menu bar. After you confirm your choice in the Caution box, the group is removed along with any program items that were in it.

| Activity 8.8 | ## Deleting Your Group |

The Documents program group window should be open on your screen. You're going to delete an item and then delete the group.

1. Delete the LOGO.BMP program item.

click the Logo icon

choose File, Delete

click Yes

The program item is removed from the Documents group.

2. Delete the Documents group.

click the Documents minimize button

click the Documents group icon

choose File, Delete

click Yes

The program group icon for the Documents group is removed from the Program Manager window.

Using the StartUp Group

When you first use Windows, the StartUp group is empty.

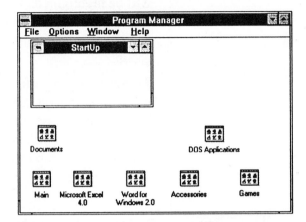

The StartUp group is provided as a means of starting applications automatically when you start Windows. Any program item that you add to the StartUp group is started whenever you start Windows.

You can add program items to the StartUp group in any of the ways you've already learned. By default, programs you add to the StartUp group will be started in a window. If you want to run an application as an icon, you can do so with the File, Properties command.

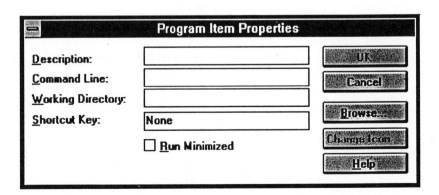

Activity 8.9

Starting Applications Automatically

1. Begin by closing any program groups.

   double-click the Control-menu box for any open groups

2. Open the StartUp group.

   double-click the StartUp group icon

3. Open another group and arrange the windows.

   select Window, Accessories

   select Window, Tile

4. Place a copy of the Clock icon in the StartUp group.

   hold down the [Ctrl] key and drag the Clock icon to the StartUp group

5. Set it up so that the Clock will run minimized.

   click the Clock icon in the StartUp group

   select File, Properties

   in the dialog box, click the Run Minimized check box

   click OK

   Now, the next time you start Windows, the Clock will start and run as an icon on the desktop.

On Your Own

1. Exit Windows and restart to see the effect of putting the Clock in the StartUp group.

2. Use drag and drop from the File Manager to put the Recorder file MYMAC.REC in the StartUp group. Make the item start and run minimized.

3. Exit Windows and restart to see the effect of your changes.

Quick Check

1. List the default program groups in Windows.

2. Which menu in the Program Manager is used to arrange program group windows and icons? Describe each choice on the menu.

3. How do you create a new program group?

4. What command do you use to add program items to a group? How else can you add items?

5. How do you delete a program item? A program group?

6. What is the purpose of the StartUp group?

Chapter
9

Working with DOS Applications

Until now, you've been working with applications that were designed and written for the Windows environment. In this chapter you'll learn how to access and manipulate non-Windows applications.

While the ideal way to work with the Windows program is to use programs that take advantage of all Windows' capabilities, it is possible to use "non-Windows" or DOS applications. DOS applications are programs designed to work with the Disk Operating System, and not specifically designed to work with Windows.

While some computer users may choose to purchase only software programs that are Windows compatible, many users have invested substantial money and time in buying and learning to use word processors, spreadsheets, databases, and other programs designed for DOS. Other users may find that they don't have sufficient hard disk space or a fast enough computer to take advantage of some of the Windows-compatible applications.

If you're going to work with DOS applications, you may find it more useful and convenient to run them "under" — that is, while using—the Windows environment. In this chapter, you'll learn how you can get the best results.

- Understand the advantages of running DOS applications under Windows

- Access DOS applications from Windows

- Run DOS applications full-screen, windowed, or minimized

- Set up new DOS applications
- Create Program Information Files for DOS applications
- Switch between DOS and Windows applications
- Cut and paste between DOS and Windows applications

Non-Windows Applications Under Windows

While programs that weren't designed for use with Windows don't share the appearance and menu system of Windows programs, there are several advantages to running these programs under Windows. *Running under Windows* simply means launching, or starting, the application when Windows is running.

When running under Windows, you can start and switch in and out of your DOS application programs just as you can start and switch in and out of Cardfile or Write. This means that:

- You don't have to save and exit a DOS program before starting another.

In addition, non-Windows applications can take over the full screen as they normally do, or they can be viewed in a smaller window with other programs visible at the same time.

And, although the capability is limited, it's possible to cut and paste information to and from a non-Windows application.

Starting a DOS Program

You can start a DOS program from the File Manager within Windows. You can't always tell by looking at the program file icon whether an application was designed for Windows or is a non-Windows application. When you start a non-Windows application, however, you will notice differences. This is because:

- Windows applications share a graphical user interface, while most non-Windows applications are character-based.

- Some non-Windows applications require input from the keyboard and don't recognize the mouse.

- Non-Windows applications appear in full-screen mode rather than in a window.

In the next activity, you'll start a DOS program called Frageval that checks your hard disk and reports on fragmentation.

Activity 9.1

Running a DOS Program

1. Open the File Manager and look at the files on the A: drive.

   double-click the Main program group

   double-click the File Manager

   click the icon for the A: drive

2. Open the \fragchek directory.

   in the left side of the window, click the fragchek directory

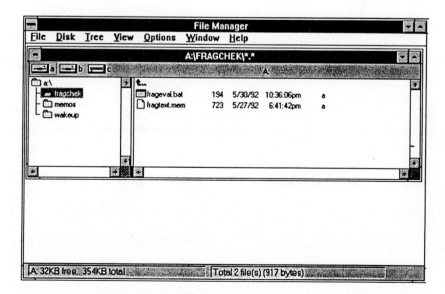

Notice that there are two files, one of which is a text file. The other has a program icon and ends with .BAT. Files that end with .BAT, .EXE, or .COM are files that make programs run.

3. Run the Frageval program to check for fragmented files on a disk.

   double-click the FRAGEVAL.BAT file

   The Frageval program will start, and—like all non-Windows applications—it will take over the full screen.

4. Follow the instructions on the screen until the program finishes.

   press a key as instructed until the program finishes

Manipulating DOS Applications

When you start a DOS application that's running in full-screen mode, you may want to place the application in its own window. You can do so by pressing [Alt] [Enter]. The program will then display in a window with a title bar, control-menu, and minimize and maximize buttons. You can manipulate the window by:

- Clicking the minimize button to shrink it to an icon.

- Pressing [Alt] [Enter] to display the application full-screen once again.

In the next activity, you'll restart the Frageval program and display it in a window.

Activity 9.2

Manipulating a DOS Window

1. Start the Frageval program.

   double-click the FRAGEVAL.BAT file

2. Place the Frageval program in a window.

   press [Alt][Enter]

3. Try to close the program from the Control-menu box.

   click the Control-menu box

   Notice that the Close option is dimmed.

   Note: DOS applications must be closed by the appropriate procedure from *within* the application.

4. Follow the instructions on the screen until the program finishes.

   press a key as instructed until the program finishes

5. Return to the C: drive.

   click the icon for the C: drive

6. Close the File Manager.

   double-click the File Manager's Control-menu box

Setting up Popular DOS Applications

The Windows Setup procedure will automatically detect most of the popular Windows and non-Windows software programs on your hard disk and create icons for them. However, it may not detect lesser-known programs such as the Frageval utility.

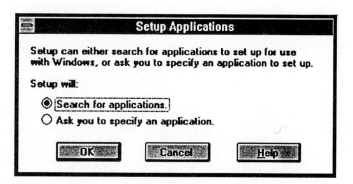

Activity 9.3

Using Setup for DOS Applications

1. Begin the procedure to automatically set up icons for popular non-Windows applications.

double-click the Windows Setup icon in the Main program group

select Options, Set Up Applications

make sure the Search for Applications option is selected

click the OK button

2. Choose to search the C: drive for applications.

click C: in the list box

if any other selections are still highlighted, click to de-select them

click Search Now

Windows will now search through your hard disk for programs it recognizes. If you are asked for the names of any programs, simply click OK to accept the suggested name.

3. If programs were found, read through the list, but don't add any new programs at this time.

click Cancel to close the window

If you had chosen to Add the programs, Windows would have automatically created icons for them in the Applications group.

4. Close the Windows Setup window.

double-click the Windows Setup Control-menu box

Program Information Files

Whenever you run a non-Windows application, Windows must have a Program Information File (PIF) for that application. Since DOS programs may have special hardware or memory requirements that Windows needs to know about, it's necessary to set up a PIF to tell Windows where the program is stored and how it should work. The PIF also contains settings that tell Windows how to run the application.

When you use Setup for DOS applications, the necessary PIF for each application is stored in the Windows directory and is used to run the application. For DOS programs that aren't found by Setup, you may need to create a PIF yourself. To create a PIF, you use the PIF Editor program, located in the Main program group.

```
┌─────────────────────────────────────────────────────────┐
│ ▤          PIF Editor - (Untitled)              ▼ ▲      │
├─────────────────────────────────────────────────────────┤
│  File   Mode   Help                                      │
│  Program Filename:    [                              ]    │
│  Window Title:        [                              ]    │
│  Optional Parameters: [                              ]    │
│  Start-up Directory:  [                              ]    │
│  Video Memory:    ◉ Text   ○ Low Graphics   ○ High Graphics │
│  Memory Requirements:  KB Required  [128]  KB Desired  [640] │
│  EMS Memory:           KB Required  [0]    KB Limit    [1024]│
│  XMS Memory:           KB Required  [0]    KB Limit    [1024]│
│  Display Usage: ◉ Full Screen       Execution: ☐ Background │
│                 ○ Windowed                     ☐ Exclusive │
│  ☒ Close Window on Exit          [ Advanced... ]          │
├─────────────────────────────────────────────────────────┤
│  Press F1 for Help on Program Filename.                   │
└─────────────────────────────────────────────────────────┘
```

Activity 9.4

Creating a PIF

1. With the Main window open, start the PIF Editor.

    double-click the PIF Editor icon

2. Put the full path (location) and name of the Frageval program in the Program Filename box.

    *type **A:\FRAGCHEK\FRAGEVAL.BAT***

3. Give an appropriate title that will appear in the Title Bar of the window when the program runs.

    [Tab] once to the Window Title box
    *type **Fragment Checker***

4. No Optional Parameters are necessary, so skip to the Start-up Directory box.

[Tab] twice

*type **A:\FRAGCHEK***

5. Indicate that you would like this program always to run in a window, not full screen.

   click the Windowed radio button

6. Save the Program Information File.

   select File, Save

   *type **FRAG.PIF***

7. Minimize the PIF Editor.

   click the Minimize button

   You have now created a PIF to run the Frageval program.

Preparing to Use the PIF

Once you've created a PIF file for your DOS application, you can start the application from the File Manager by double-clicking the PIF. To make your application more accessible, you'll probably want to make an icon for it. You use the Program Manager File, New command to make a program group and item.

Activity 9.5

Making a Program Item for the PIF

1. With the Program Manager open, minimize any open program groups.

   click the Minimize button on all open program groups

   There should be nothing visible in the Program Manager window except the program icons at the bottom.

2. Create a new program group called Utilities.

   select File, New

   click OK

*type **Utilities***

click OK

3. Create an icon for the FRAG.PIF in the Utilities window.

select File, New

click OK

4. Type a description.

*type **Fragment Checker***

5. Fill in the Command Line box with the name of the PIF.

[Tab] once

*type **FRAG.PIF***

click OK

You should now have an icon from which to start the program.

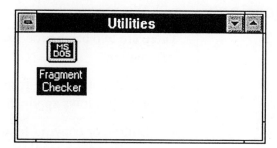

Activity 9.6 | **Using the PIF**

1. Test the PIF.

double-click the new icon

The FRAGEVAL.BAT program should run correctly.

2. Finish the Frageval program.

press keys as instructed until the program finishes and the window closes

On Your Own

1. Use the File Manager to locate the WAKEUP.EXE program on your A: drive. Make a written note of the full path and filename for use in the "Program Filename" section of your PIF.

2. Use the PIF editor to create an appropriate Program Information File. Save it and call it WAKE.PIF.

3. Use File, New to create another icon in the Utilities group for WAKE.PIF.

4. Double-click to test the new icon.

5. Close the Wakeup program by typing [N] in response to the Yes/No question at the bottom of the screen.

Cutting and Pasting between DOS Applications

Some cutting and pasting is possible with non-Windows applications. The capabilities are limited, however, and may be even further limited if you're using a network. The cut or copied text may require more editing than it would with Windows applications.

There are two basic processes to capture and paste information:

- Cutting or copying from a Windows application **to** a non-Windows application

- Cutting or copying **from** a non-Windows application to a Windows application

Copying to a DOS Application

Of these processes, the more effective and flexible is cutting and copying **to** a non-Windows application. This procedure includes the following steps:

- Open the Windows application (for example, the Cardfile), and retrieve or type the text you'll want to copy.

- Highlight the text and select Edit, Copy.

- Use [Alt][Tab] to reach the Program Manager.

- Open the non-Windows application (for example, Quattro or WordPerfect 5.1) and place the cursor where you would like the pasted text to appear.

- If the non-Windows application is not already in a window, press [Alt][Enter].

- Click the non-Windows application's Control-menu box.

- Select Edit, Paste.

Activity 9.7

Copying to a Non-Windows Application

Caution: Copying to a DOS application requires that the application have editing capabilities. If you don't have a program with such capabilities, you may not be able to try out this procedure.

1. Open the Cardfile, and retrieve the text you'll want to copy.

   double-click the Cardfile icon

   select File, Open

   click A: in the drives list

   double-click ADDRESS.CRD

2. Highlight the address on the first card and copy it.

   hold down the [Shift] key and press the down arrow three times

   select Edit, Copy

3. Return to the Program Manager.

   use [Alt][Tab] to select the Program Manager

4. Open the non-Windows application (for example, Quattro or WordPerfect 5.1) and place the cursor where you would like the pasted text to appear.

   double-click the icon for the Non-Windows application

5. If the non-Windows application is currently running full-screen, place it in a window.

if necessary, press [Alt][Enter]

6. Paste the text.

click the non-Windows application's Control-menu box

select Edit, Paste

Copying from a DOS Application

The process to copy from a non-Windows application is somewhat less flexible. It doesn't let you highlight specific text. You must copy all the information on the screen. The process includes the following steps:

- Open the DOS application, and be sure that the program is running **full screen**, not in a window.

- Depending which keys are available on your keyboard, use either the [Print Screen] key or the [Shift][PrtScr] key combination to copy the information to RAM.

- Minimize the DOS application program.

- Open the Windows program.

- Select Edit, Paste.

Activity 9.8

Copying from a Non-Windows Application

Suppose you wish to edit and print out the report on disk fragmentation that appears in the Frageval program. You can edit this material with the Notepad program, but first you must copy the information to the Notepad.

Caution: This procedure may not work on networked computers.

1. With the Utilities window open, run the Frageval program.

double-click the Frageval icon

2. Press a key to clear the explanation screen and begin the evaluation of the disk.

3. To copy from a DOS application, that program must be running **full screen**, not in a window. Change to full screen view.

   press [Alt][Enter]

4. When the report on disk quality appears, use the appropriate keys for your keyboard to copy the information to RAM.

   press the [Print Screen] or [Shift][PrtScr] key

5. Minimize the Frageval program.

   press [Alt] [Enter]
   click the Minimize button

6. Close the Utilities window, open the Accessories window, and start the Notepad.

   click the Minimize button on the Utilities window
   double-click the Accessories icon
   double-click the Notepad icon

7. Paste the text from Frageval.

   select Edit, Paste

   If desired, you may edit and print the pasted text.

Activity 9.9

Using the DOS Prompt

There aren't many file management procedures that can't be done with the Windows File Manager. But occasionally, it may be necessary to temporarily leave Windows to perform a function that only the Disk Operating System can do. Such functions include seeing the names of all the files in a directory at once, backing up a whole directory of your hard disk onto several floppy disks, running a batch file, or canceling a network print job. To perform these functions, you may have to use the DOS prompt.

1.   With the Main window open, start the MS-DOS Prompt.

     double-click the MS-DOS Prompt icon

     Read the instructions at the top of the screen for managing use of the DOS Prompt.

2.   Get a directory listing of file names going across the full width of the screen.

     *type **DIR /W/P** and press [Enter]*

     if necessary, press a key to read the rest of the listing

     While you don't get information about the dates or contents of the files as you would in File Manager, you can see more names at a glance.

3.   Close the MS-DOS Prompt.

     *type **EXIT** and press [Enter]*

On Your Own

1.   Restart the MS-DOS Prompt.

2.   Get a wide directory listing with DIR /W/P.

3.   If you're not on a network, use the Print Screen procedure to copy the wide file listing into RAM.

4.   Open the Notepad program.

5.   Use Edit, Paste to copy the information to the Notepad.

Quick Check

1. Answer the following questions, true or false.

   _____You can only run DOS applications full screen from Windows.

   _____Windows requires PIF files to run DOS applications.

   _____You can create PIF files with the Windows PIF Editor.

2. What is the purpose of a PIF file?

3. How can you change the display of DOS applications running under Windows?

4. How can you switch between DOS applications and Windows?

5. When might you use the DOS prompt icon?

Chapter
10

Sharing Information Between Applications

Overview

You've seen how Windows' Clipboard lets you cut and paste within a single application and between two applications. You've also seen that graphics as well as text can be cut, copied, or pasted. But, useful as it is, this capability isn't the limit of Windows' ability to share information between programs.

Windows also provides a powerful facility for sharing information among applications. This facility is known as Object Linking and Embedding (OLE). Within Windows, you can use several applications—such as the Paintbrush, Sound Recorder, Write, and Cardfile—to share information in this way. Another Windows Accessory, the Object Packager, provides special OLE services. Other applications that run under Windows—Microsoft Word 2.0 and Excel 4.0, for example, and Ami Pro 2.0—also support OLE.

This chapter introduces the concepts and terminology of OLE, describes the difference between linking and embedding, and illustrates the techniques for doing both.

Objectives

- Understand the concepts of Object Linking and Embedding (OLE)

- Understand the difference between linking and embedding

- Identify the menu commands for linking and embedding

- Embed an object in a Windows document

- Link an object from one Windows document to another

- Insert an object as a package in a Windows document

- Use the File Manager to insert an object package

- Use the Object Packager to create packages

What Is OLE?

OLE is a powerful way of transferring and sharing data between Windows applications. The data that is shared is called an object. An **object** is any information created with a Windows application. It may be text, graphics, charts, sound, or a package that represents one of these. An object may be a single cell of a spreadsheet or an entire document.

OLE allows you to "link" and "embed" objects from one application into another. This means you can create documents that contain data from a variety of applications. Moreover, you can edit any of the data from within your current document, by opening one application from within another.

Here's a simple, practical example. Suppose that you have to prepare a monthly report that includes a graph and a spreadsheet in addition to text. If the graph and spreadsheet are embedded objects, you can open them from within the report, make changes to them, and continue working in the report.

To understand OLE, you'll need to be familiar with the concepts and terminology described in the following pages.

Servers and Clients

An application used to create and edit an object is called a **server**, also referred to as the **source**. An application that receives and stores the object is called a **client**, also known as the **destination**. An application that supports OLE may be either a server or a client, or in some cases both.

- Paintbrush and Sound Recorder are OLE servers (sources).

- Write and Cardfile are clients (destinations).

- Other applications like Microsoft Word and Excel can be both server/sources and client/destinations.

When a drawing from Paintbrush is embedded in a Write document, Paintbrush is the server application, and Write is the client. If an Excel spreadsheet is embedded in a Word document, Excel is the server, and Word is the client.

Note: Windows includes the programming that makes OLE available as well as several Accessories that support OLE. To support OLE, other applications must be written to take advantage of the included technology. Check the application's documentation to see if it supports OLE.

Linking or Embedding

When you **link** an object, you copy information from the server to the client without making a physical copy of the data in the client document. Instead of a copy of the object, the destination document contains a link which is a "pointer" to the original source document. For example, suppose you're writing a memo which mentions the expenses for a project. The expenses are being calculated with a spreadsheet program such as Lotus or Excel, but additional bills may still come in. Rather than changing your memo each time an additional expense is added to the spreadsheet, you could create a link which will show the latest information from the spreadsheet automatically.

- To edit a linked object, you must have access to the original source file.

- A change in the source is immediately reflected in the destination.

When you **embed** an object, all the information that would normally be stored in the server application is stored in the file created by the client application. Multiple embedded objects (from the same or different server applications) can be stored in a single file. For example, suppose you are now writing a memo which makes suggestions for next year's budget. You are going to base your budget estimates on last year's expenses, which were calculated with a spreadsheet program. But you don't want to alter the spreadsheet which contains the expenses! And you don't want the budget portion of your memo to disappear when the accounting department closes out the books and removes last year's expense information from the computer. In this case, you could embed a copy of the information which will be independent of the original spreadsheet file.

- To edit an embedded object, you do not need the original source file, only the application that created it.

- A change in the source is not reflected in the destination.

Whether to link or embed depends on how you plan to use and update the source and the destination documents, as shown in the table below.

Use Linking If:	Use Embedding If:
You want to maintain a single copy of information to which several clients are linked.	A centralized data source is not necessary, or data may be altered only in the destination document.
The source document will be available to all users of the destination document and will not be moved.	Users will not have access to the source document if source or OLE client file is moved.
The client application supports linking, but not embedding.	Users of the destination document will not have access to the source document.

Embedding an Object

There are two ways you can begin to embed an object.

One way is to start from the source application. If you begin from the source application, you use the Edit, Copy command to place the object on the Clipboard. Then, in the destination application, you use Edit, Paste to embed the object.

| **Activity 10.1** | **Embedding a Paintbrush Drawing** |

In this activity, you'll embed a Paintbrush drawing in a Write document. To begin, you'll start Paint.

1. Start the Paint program and maximize the window.

    double-click Paint in the Accessories group
    click the maximize button

2. Open a file containing the object.

    select File, Open
    click A: in the drives list
    double-click ACME.BMP

3. Place the object on the Clipboard and close Paintbrush.

    use the Pick tool to select the ACME graphic
    choose Edit, Copy
    double-click the Control-menu box
    You're now ready to start Write and embed the object.

4. Start the Write program and maximize the window.

    double-click Write in the Accessories group
    click the maximize button

5. Open a file and position the cursor.

    select File, Open
    click A: in the drives list
    double-click ACME.WRI
    move the insertion point above the address

6.   Embed the object.

select Edit, Paste

The drawing is placed in your Write document.

Once an object is embedded, it can be edited.

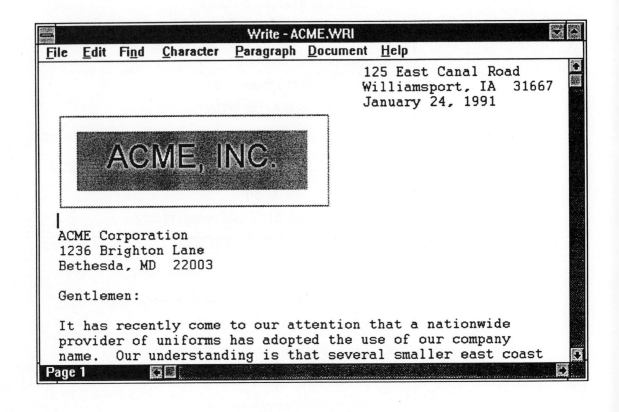

Activity 10.2 | ## Editing an Embedded Object

1. Edit the drawing from within Write.

double-click the graphic in the document

Paintbrush begins with the object ready for editing. Notice the title bar of the Paintbrush window.

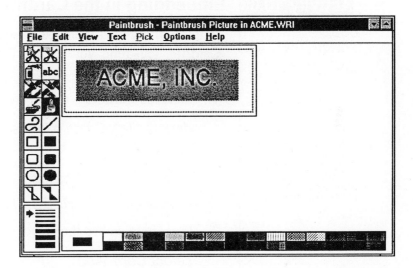

2. Add something to the drawing.

use the circle tool to draw a circle around the company name

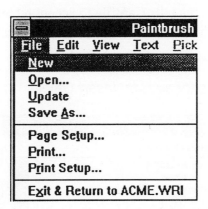

3. Update the drawing.

choose File, Update

4. Return to Write.

choose File, Exit & Return to ACME.WRI

The graphic is updated in your Write document.

Another way to embed an object is to start the destination application. If you begin from the destination application, you use the Edit, Insert Object command to start the procedure. All the installed applications that support OLE are then listed in a dialog box for you to choose from.

Activity 10.3 Embedding in the Cardfile

In this activity, you'll embed a Paintbrush drawing in a Cardfile. This time, you'll begin from the destination application.

1.   Start the Cardfile program and open a file.

double-click Cardfile in the Accessories group

select File, Open

click A: in the drives list

double-click ADDRESS.CRD

2.   Prepare to embed the object.

select Card, Add

*type **ACME, Inc.***

click OK

choose Edit, Picture

This tells Cardfile to accept pictures. The picture will be placed in the upper left corner of the card.

3.   Begin to insert the object.

choose Edit, Insert Object

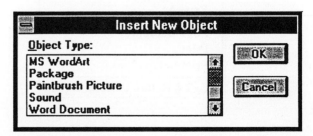

in the dialog box choose Paintbrush Picture

click OK

Paintbrush begins.

4. Get the ACME.BMP graphic.

    select Edit, Paste From

    click A: in the drives list

    double-click ACME.BMP

5. Embed the object and return to the Cardfile.

    select File, Update

    select File, Exit & Return to ADDRESS.CRD

    The drawing is placed in your Cardfile.

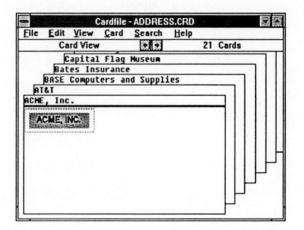

On Your Own

1. Add another card to the Cardfile and embed the LOGO.BMP file on it.

2. Edit the LOGO.BMP and return to the Cardfile.

3. Save the changes and close the Cardfile.

Linking an Object

Instead of embedding, you may choose to create a link from the source application to the destination document. When you create a link, an image of the object appears in the destination document, but there is no physical copy of the data in that document. Instead, there is a link — or pointer — between the source and destination.

- Any changes in the source file appear in any document that contains a link to the source.

    Note: You must have saved the file that contains the object to be linked.

You can edit the linked object from the destination document, and you do so just the way you edit an embedded object.

Activity 10.4

Creating a Link to a Paintbrush Drawing

In this activity, you'll link a Paintbrush drawing to a Write document. To begin, you'll start Paint.

1. Start the Paint program and maximize the window.

    double-click Paint in the Accessories group

    click the maximize button

2. Open the file containing the object.

    select File, Open

    click A: in the drives list

    double-click ART.BMP

3. Place the object on the Clipboard and minimize Paintbrush.

    use the Pick tool to select one of the graphics

    choose Edit, Copy

    click the minimize button

    You're now ready to start Write and link to the object.

4. Start the Write program and maximize the window.

    double-click Write in the Accessories group

    click the maximize button

5. Open a file and position the cursor.

select File, Open

click A: in the drives list

double-click ARTMEMO.WRI

move the insertion point between the two paragraphs

6. Link the object.

select Edit, Paste Link

The drawing is placed in your Write document, and is linked to the source.

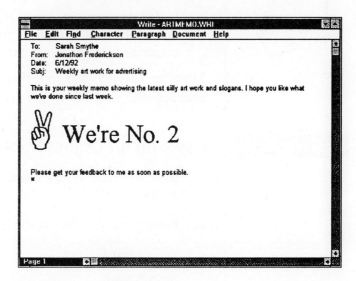

On Your Own

1. Create a link to the other graphic in the ART.BMP file.

2. Edit the graphic and return to Write.

3. Save the changes and close Write.

Object Packages

You've seen that when you embed or link an object into another document, the object appears in the destination document as it does in the source application. In another method of linking and embedding, you can embed or link icons that represent objects in a destination document. These icons are called **packages.**

- A package may contain either a link or an embedded object.

- A package itself is always embedded and has the same properties as an embedded object.

You can use a package any place you might want to embed an object. Suppose, for example, you wanted to create a document that referenced another report. Rather than include the report in its entirety, you might embed an icon representing the report.

Note: You can only insert packages into applications that support OLE. Check the application's documentation to see if it does.

There are several ways to embed an object package. In the next activity, you'll drag and drop from the File Manager.

Activity 10.5

Inserting an Object Package

1. Run the Write program and open the file A:\TEXT.WRI.

2. Place the cursor below the name Greer.

    select Find, Find

    type Greer

    press [Enter]

    click the Cancel button

    press the down arrow on the keyboard

3. Open the File Manager and find the file called TRAINING.WRI.

    from the Main window, double-click File Manager

    select the root directory of the A: drive

choose File, Search

type TRAINING.WRI

click OK

4. Arrange the windows so that you can see both the File Manager and Write.

   drag the File Manager window

   drag the Write window

5. Copy the icon to the space below the name "Greer."

   drag the icon for TRAINING.WRI to the space below "Greer" in the Write window

   You'll see a Write icon inside of the TEXT.WRI document.

6. Type an explanation for the icon.

   below the icon, type USE THIS ICON TO SEE COURSE INFORMATION

On Your Own

1. Double-click the Write icon embedded in your document.

   What happens?

2. Save your file and close Write.

Using the Object Packager

The Object Packager — an application supplied with Windows — lets you create and insert object packages in destination documents. Using the Object Packager, you can package an entire document or a part of a document.

You can also customize the icon that represents the object and change its label.

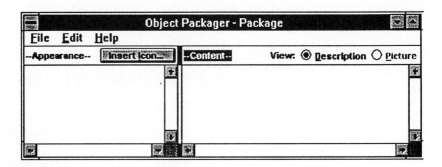

<table>
</table>

| **Activity 10.6** | **Packaging an Object** |

1. Start the Object Packager program.

double-click Object Packager in the Accessories group

2. Get the contents of the package.

select the Content window
choose File, Import
click A: in the Drives list
double-click ART.BMP

3. Start Cardfile and open a file.

double-click Cardfile
choose File, Open
click A: in the drives list
double-click ADDRESS.CRD

4. Prepare to insert the package.

select Card, Add
*type **Art work***
click OK

5. Arrange the windows so you can see the Cardfile and Object Packager.

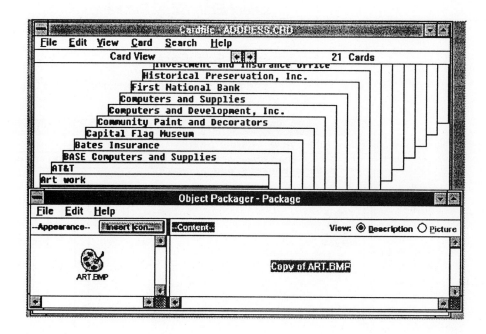

double-click on the desktop

in the Task List, select Object Packager

click Switch To

You should be able to see the Object Packager on top of the Cardfile.

6. Insert ART.BMP into the Cardfile.

click in the Object Packager window

select Edit, Copy Package

click in the Cardfile

select Edit, Paste

The object package is inserted in the Cardfile.

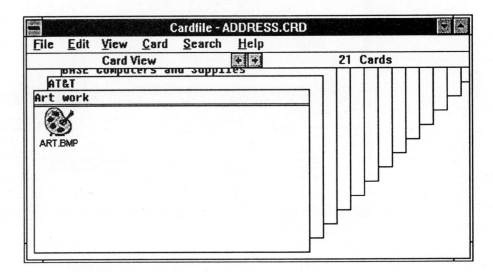

Quick Check

1. What is OLE?

2. Match the following terms:

   _____ server   a.   destination

   _____ client   b.   information

   _____ object   c.   source

3. When would you use linking? When would you use embedding?

4. What menu contains commands for OLE?

5. List the commands and their function.

6. How can you insert an object from the File Manager?

Appendix
A

The Computer System

In little more than ten years, the personal computer has revolutionized the organization, processing, and production of information in schools, offices, hospitals, factories, stores, and even homes. To understand these modern techniques for organizing information, it is necessary to be familiar with personal computers and how they work.

To learn about computers, you will need to know a bit about *hardware*, or the physical components of the machine. In addition, you will need to know about *software*, or the computer programs that manage the machine.

One of the most popular and powerful programs for personal computers is Microsoft Windows. This software program revolutionized information processing further by enabling more advanced manipulation of procedures and data. To be in step with some of the latest advances in computer usage, you should become familiar with the Windows program.

This appendix will help you to:

• Be familiar with the hardware components of a computer system.

• Appreciate the importance and purpose of computer memory.

• Understand the types and uses of input/output devices.

• Be acquainted with the capabilities of computer networking.

• Identify the broad categories of computer software available today.

- Be familiar with various types of application software and understand the uses of each type in the workplace.

- Understand the importance of operating systems in the computer environment.

Computer Hardware

A computer is a system, made up of three basic parts: hardware, input/output devices (also known as peripherals), and software. None of these parts is of any use without the others.

The term *hardware* generally refers to the computer box, or chassis, and the electronic components it houses. These components include:

- Central Processing Unit

- Chips

- Boards or Adapter Cards

CPU

The Central Processing Unit (**CPU**) interprets and processes data based on instructions written by human beings. The CPU is a chip — a piece of silicon in which an integrated electronic circuit is formed.

The type of CPU chip in a computer determines its power and speed of processing. Original IBM personal computers used an Intel 8088 chip. Newer, faster, and more powerful computers use the 80286 chip (IBM AT and compatible computers); they are often called 286 computers. Faster still are 386 and even 486 machines, using 80386 and 80486 CPU chips. To use Windows (Version 3.1 or higher) you must have an 80286 or better chip.

CPU chips, and other types of chips, are small black rectangles with protruding prongs. The prongs fit securely into holes on *boards*, or *adapter cards*. The main board in a computer is called the motherboard, the master circuit board into which the CPU chip and other chips are inserted.

In addition to the CPU chip, the motherboard has slots, into which can be inserted special-purpose boards that contain chips designed to control additional functions or pieces of equipment. Attached to some of these boards, and extending through openings in the back of the chassis, are outlets, called ports, into which peripherals such as printers or monitors can be plugged. Thus every part of the computer is directly or indirectly connected to the motherboard, and every action taken by the computer is directly or indirectly controlled by the CPU.

Memory

Computer memory is also composed of chips, some on the motherboard and possibly more on *memory expansion boards*. Memory is the electronic area that contains the active instructions (programs) telling the CPU what to do, and the data to be processed.

There are two kinds of computer memory: ROM and RAM.

ROM — Read-Only Memory — is a chip containing built-in, always-present instructions that control the basic functioning of the computer, including the directions that enable the computer to *boot*, or start up. The instructions in ROM are read and carried out automatically by the CPU with no action required on the part of the user.

RAM — Random Access Memory — is the memory, also contained in chips, that is used as the work area of the computer. When your computer is turned off, RAM is empty. To use the computer, you gather the tools (programs) you need and *load* them into RAM. You also *input* (type) your *data* (words, numbers, drawings) into RAM. The CPU responds to the keys you type and the instructions within the loaded program to manipulate the data in RAM.

When your work is complete, you use another program, DOS, to send it to a printer, or to store it safely away, moving it from RAM where it was created to a permanent storage area of your computer. That same program, DOS, is used to retrieve a copy of your project, or *file*, back into RAM when you need to read or work on it again.

RAM has a finite capacity, which is measured in units called kilobytes. A byte, abbreviated b, is the amount of space occupied by one typed character. Kilo, abbreviated K, comes from the Greek word for 1000. A kilobyte, or Kb, is the amount of space required to store 1000 characters. A computer with 640Kb RAM can handle 640,000 characters of programs and data at one time in memory.

To use Windows 3.1, your computer must have at least one megabyte (million-character capacity) of RAM. Two or more megabytes are recommended. Additional memory comes in the form of chips inserted into either the motherboard, if there is room, or on memory expansion boards plugged into the motherboard.

The more RAM a computer has, the more and bigger programs it can work with, and the more room it has to receive and manipulate data. Just as your productivity slows down if your desk is too cluttered, computer performance slows down without enough memory.

Input Devices

Input/output (I/O) devices, or peripherals, enable the user to get data into RAM for processing, and to get the results of that processing out of RAM for viewing or other use.

Input devices include:

- Keyboards
- Mice
- Scanners, digitizers, CD-ROM, lightpens, voice synthesizers

Keyboard

The keyboard is the basic input device. It is used to type instructions and data into RAM for the computer to process. Keyboards have several sections:

Typewriter Keypad

The standard letters, numbers, symbols, and spacebar keys that are found on a regular typewriter. These keys perform as expected regardless of which program you are using.

They are found on the central section of the computer keyboard.

Software-Specific Keys

Some keys that are usually found on a standard typewriter may perform differently on a computer than when pressed on a typewriter. These keys include [Backspace], [Tab], and [Shift]. These and other central-section keys such as [Ctrl] (control), [Alt] (alternate), and [Esc] (escape) are *software specific* — what they do depends on which program is being used.

Function Keys

The 10 or 12 F keys are across the top of extended keyboards or to the left side of standard keyboards. These keys are software-specific and are used to issue commands to programs to perform particular functions.

Numeric Keypad

Number keys are arranged in an adding-machine format on the far right side of the computer keyboard. On some keyboards, you must press the [NumLock] key above the numeral 7 before using the keypad to type numbers. The [+], [-], [*], and [/] keys around the outside of the keypad are the arithmetic operators; the [Enter] key functions like [Enter] in the main typewriter keypad.

Arrow and Editing Keys

On extended 101-key keyboards there is a separate cursor-control keypad consisting of arrows in all four directions and [Insert], [Delete], [Home], [End], [PageUp] and [PageDown]. On standard (84-key) keyboards these keys are on the numeric keypad keys along with the numerals and decimal point. These keys move the cursor (blinking underline) over data on the screen and enable adding (inserting) and erasing (deleting) data for editing purposes. On standard keyboards, if [NumLock] is not pressed, the numeric keypad can be used as the cursor-control and editing keypad.

Toggles

[NumLock] and [CapsLock] are toggles — pressing them once turns them on, or engages them; pressing them a second time turns them off. [NumLock] switches the numeric keypad between typing numbers and moving the cursor. [CapsLock] toggles uppercase letters on and off.

Mouse

A mouse is a point-and-shoot input device that moves a pointer across the screen as the mouse is moved across a desktop. Mice have two or three buttons (whose functions are software-specific) that are clicked to select the item the pointer is pointing to. Many programs today, including Windows, are mouse-compatible; other programs cannot use a mouse as an input device.

Other Input Devices

A great number of new types of input devices are coming to market. These technologically remarkable devices attempt to make entering data into RAM easier or more convenient.

- **Scanners** can read a printed page into the computer with no typing required.

- **Digitizers** can scan a drawing into the computer where it can then be edited.

- **CD-ROMs** allow vast amounts of pre-recorded data on compact disks to be selectively retrieved into the computer.

- **Lightpens** and **touch screens** enable the user to shine a light on or touch a part of the screen to make a choice from displayed selections.

- **Voice synthesizers** automatically type words on the screen as they are spoken into a microphone.

These and other input devices are part of the future of personal computing.

Output Devices

To interact with a computer, you must be able to see what is going on in RAM. There must be ways to *output* to the user the data that is in memory. Output devices receive electronically transmitted images from RAM in a form that the user can interpret. Output devices include:

- Monitors
- Printers

Monitor

A monitor, or computer screen, lets you view what is happening in the computer's work area, RAM. When you type characters, they are input into RAM and you see them on the monitor.

The monitor is cabled to a *video adapter card* which is plugged into a slot on the motherboard. The chips on the card control the functioning of the video display within the limits of the capabilities of the monitor — how many colors can be produced (from one color on a black background to 256 or more throughout the spectrum); the screen resolution (how sharp the images appear); and whether graphic images can be produced.

Types of monitor/video adapter card combinations include:

- Monochrome text only (one-color display, no graphics).

- Monochrome or color graphics.

- EGA (enhanced graphics adapter) color or monochrome graphics with good resolution.

- VGA (video graphics array) color or monochrome graphics with excellent resolution.

Because the Windows program is a graphical user interface, you will need a monitor with graphics capabilities.

Printer

The contents of RAM can also be output to a printer. Printers vary in speed and quality of output depending on the mechanism used to produce the printed characters. Like monitors, some printers can produce graphic characters. Some can print in color.

Printers are cabled to printer ports, sockets connected to printer adapter cards and extending from the back of the computer chassis. Data from RAM is sent to the printer port and retrieved by the printer in one of two ways, depending on the type of port.

- *Serial ports* receive data in a series of electronic impulses (bits), one after another, to define a single character to be printed. Serial ports are identified as COM1, COM2, etc.

- *Parallel ports* process, as a unit of parallel impulses, all the bits that make up a single character. While parallel transmission is faster, it can only be used with cables less than 15 ft. long. Parallel ports are LPT1, LPT2, etc. Printer port LPT1 is the default, or assumed, printer port.

If you instruct your system to output data to a printer, unless you specify otherwise, the data will be sent to the printer that is plugged into the LPT1 printer port.

Dot-matrix Printers

Dot-matrix printers use a series of pins hitting a typewriter-like ribbon to create a character as a pattern of dots. The more pins, and the more closely spaced the dots, the higher the resolution (sharpness) of the character. Printing speed is measured in characters-per-second.

Laser Printers

Laser printers — more expensive, faster, and quieter than dot matrix printers — produce images by spraying powdered toner onto a piece of paper which passes over a heating element that fuses the powder. Resolution of the output is high. An entire page is produced as a single unit, unlike the character-by-character output of a dot matrix printer. Printing speed is measured in pages-per-minute.

Daisy Wheel Printers

Daisy wheel printers have a plastic disk, or wheel, with letters and numbers on the ends of the "petals." To print, this wheel spins around, and the characters impact on a ribbon against the paper. While the print quality is fairly good, this is not an ideal printer for use with the Windows program because it cannot produce graphical elements.

Other types of equipment produce output on paper. Ink-jet printers finely spray a pattern of ink onto paper. Plotters use colored markers to draw output. Thermal printers use a heat process.

Dual I/O Devices

Two types of devices can be used both to load data into RAM and to receive data out of RAM:

- Modems
- Disk drives

Modem

A modem is a device that connects your computer to a telephone line, enabling you to dial up and communicate with another computer also connected to a modem. Data can be *downloaded* into your RAM from the other computer, or *uploaded* from your RAM to the other computer. Modems are often used to communicate with electronic bulletin boards — programs running on remote computers that enable you to receive business, educational, or recreational information.

Disk Drives

A disk drive functions like a tape recorder/player. It magnetically records data from RAM onto a disk like a tape recorder records music on a tape. It can retrieve or play back that data into RAM like a tape player can play back a song over and over again.

Disks are the permanent storage medium of the computer system. They act as file cabinets to store data created and manipulated in RAM. The contents of RAM are erased whenever your computer is turned off. Data stored on disks, however, remains there permanently, or until you decide to remove it if it is no longer needed.

There are two kinds of disk drives: hard (or fixed) disk drives, and floppy disk drives. A **hard disk drive** contains a permanently installed hard disk, which looks like a thick 45-rpm record. **Floppy disk drives** read from and write to floppy disks. Floppies are thin (.003-.005 inches), flexible, polyethylene 3-1/2"- or 5-1/4"-diameter circles with a magnetic oxide coating, encased in either a hard plastic cartridge or heavy-coated-paper jacket. Floppy disks are portable; they can be inserted and removed from disk drives as needed.

The capacity of a hard disk, measured in megabytes (millions of characters of storage space), is larger than that of floppies (usually measured in kilobytes of storage space). Hard disk drives record (write) and play back (read) data faster than floppy drives.

A computer system usually has at least one hard drive and one floppy drive. The drives are referred to by letters followed by a colon (:). The hard drive is usually called C:. The floppy drive is A:. An additional floppy drive would be designated B:. Extra hard drives would be D:, E:, etc.

Caring for Disks

All of the equipment discussed so far has one purpose: to enable you to create usable information. In effect, the most important part of the computer system is a disk, because that is what is used to save the data you create.

Hard disks are somewhat protected from damage by being permanently installed inside the computer chassis. Floppy disks, however, are subject to damage and environmental contamination from such sources as physical scratches, dust, moisture, magnetic fields (produced by televisions, ringing telephones, computer monitors), and extreme temperatures. If a disk is damaged, the data stored on it may be unusable. The following basic rules must be observed when handling floppy disks to ensure their safety:

- Never touch the exposed magnetic surface of the disk. (On a 5-1/4" disk, the magnetic surface is visible through the oval opening. On a 3-1/2" disk, the surface is exposed when the shutter on the plastic cartridge slides open.)

- Use a felt-tipped pen to write on disk labels. Never create more than one layer of labels on a disk.

- Store disks in a place protected from direct sunlight, heat, and magnetic fields.

- Keep 5-1/4" disks in a protective paper sleeve when not in use.

Inserting Disks

To correctly insert disks into disk drives:

5-1/4" disk — The edge with the exposed oval is inserted first, with the stapled edges of the jacket to the bottom or rear. Some 5-1/4" drives have a lever which must be turned down or to the side to lock the disk in place; turn it up or to the side carefully to release the disk for removal.

3-1/2" disk — The metal shutter is inserted first, with the round metal circle to the bottom or rear. Insert the disk into the disk drive until you feel it catch or hear a click. Release the disk by pushing the button on the front of the drive.

Write Protection

To protect the data on the disk from being changed or erased, cover the write-protect notch on the side of a 5-1/4" disk with a small piece of tape (usually sold with the disks), or open the write-protect hole of a 3-1/2" disk by sliding up the built-in tab. To store information on a write-protected disk, remove the tape or close the hole.

Network Resources

Your computer, and everything inside it and physically connected to it, is a **local resource**. A local resource is a tool usable only by the person actually sitting at the computer that houses it.

Local Area Networks (**LANs**) are systems that employ network adapter cards, cables, and special instructions to join multiple computers together. One or more of the linked computers is a *server*, a computer that shares its resources — disk drives, printers, modems, scanners — with all the other computers on the network. This ability to share sophisticated equipment broadens the usefulness of the individual computer beyond its own limited resources

Computer Software

Software, also known as computer programs, is a set of detailed step-by-step instructions that provides the computer with all the information it needs to perform a task, such as calculation of numeric values or manipulation of words on a page. Programs interpret the information you input with a keyboard or mouse or other input device, and then direct the CPU to carry out a procedure. Different kinds of software perform different kinds of tasks.

Loading Programs

Software is usually purchased on floppy disks. The instructions that make up the programs are magnetically recorded on the disk. These instructions can sometimes be used directly from the floppy disk. Often, the programs are too large to fit on just one disk, so they are installed on the hard disk for convenience.

A command is typed to load the program into RAM, from either the hard disk or the floppy disk, so the CPU can read it. Loading a program is like listening to a song on a tape. You hear a copy of the song; the act of playing it doesn't remove the original from the tape. An electronic copy of a program is loaded into RAM; the original remains on the disk so it can be loaded again and again.

Programs are often referred to as *software packages*. The package includes the disk or disks on which are stored the program itself and any auxiliary files the program needs, as well as documentation or instructions for using the program. Also included in the package might be templates—cardboard maps of how the software-specific keys function with the program. Registration information may also be included in the package. Registering software identifies you as a rightful user of the program. Most programs, like books, are copyrighted. It is illegal to duplicate them without permission.

Categories of Software

Software is like recipes — detailed instructions for accomplishing a goal. There are several broad categories of software. Within each category are a number of different kinds of programs. And many software developers have created unique, though similar, versions of each type of program.

Applications — Programs that apply the power of the computer system to a specific task such as word processing, database management, or communications.

Languages — Programs with special vocabulary and syntax that facilitate the writing of other programs in a way that the CPU can interpret them and a person can use them.

Utilities or Environments — Programs that generally create no data themselves, but that enhance the usefulness of other programs.

Operating Systems — Programs that control the flow of information between the various parts of the computer system. All other software must be used in conjunction with an operating system.

Applications

When you think of using a computer, you are probably thinking of using an application. You have a specific task in mind, such as typing a letter. The computer itself, the CPU, knows nothing about indenting paragraphs or underlining phrases or changing margins. The CPU must read detailed instructions in RAM about performing each of those procedures. Such instructions come from an application program.

In general, each type of application enables you to work with one kind of data. To work with textual data, you would load into RAM a word processing application. To create presentation-quality charts and graphs you would load a graphics application.

Types of application software include:

- Word processors
- Electronic spreadsheets
- Database management systems
- Graphics
- Desktop publishers
- Communications

Word Processors

Word processing software makes up a large part of all software sold. It enables a writer to input text and then make instant editing changes. Characters, words, sentences, and paragraphs can be inserted, deleted or moved without retyping. There are many word processing packages on the market. They all perform basic editing operations.

Text can be *enhanced* by most word processors — underlined, boldfaced (made darker for emphasis), automatically centered on a page — or *formatted* to appear in columns or double-spaced. Word processors also facilitate the printing of documents to user specifications: number of copies, page margins, character appearance (font).

Many word processors include spelling checkers, table editors for formatting charts of text, and *merge* capabilities which let a standard letter be individually addressed to a number of different people.

Documents created by a word processor — or by any application program — can be saved on a disk and later played back or retrieved to be re-read, edited, or printed again.

Electronic Spreadsheets

Spreadsheet applications are electronic versions of a standard ledger used for decades in accounting and budgeting procedures.

The spreadsheet is a table of intersecting rows and columns. The rectangles produced by the intersections are called *cells*. Data — text or values — is entered into cells. Contents of cells can be copied or moved. Values can be arithmetically manipulated. Powerful formulas can be entered into cells that relate values to each other. Changes made in one portion of the spreadsheet can be reflected in formulas throughout the spreadsheet. Such relationships among values make it possible to make "what-if" projections.

Spreadsheets can be used to store tables of data such as personnel records. They are often used to make budget projections based on different variables. They facilitate calculations of totals and percentages, as well as complicated functions such as mortgage amortization and standard deviation.

Database Management Systems

A database is an organized collection of information, such as a library card catalog, a telephone book, or a Rolodex file. Database management involves adding, changing, looking up, organizing, and removing information from the database.

A computer database management system enables you to store and manage vast amounts of information electronically. Database applications are used extensively for mailing list maintenance, inventory control, accounting and bookkeeping procedures, and bibliography management.

Once the form or structure of the database has been determined, and the data entered into that structure, the user can rearrange (sort), query (look up), change, add, remove, and print information in the database in many ways.

Graphics

Graphics programs extend the capability of the computer system beyond just working with words and numbers. When used with monitors and printers capable of displaying graphic characters, these programs can create original artwork, charts, and graphs based on numeric values calculated with spreadsheet or database software.

Some graphics packages enable the user to produce free-hand drawings or to use pre-defined shapes to create pictures. Many such programs come with a library of *clip-art images*, complete electronic drawings that can be edited or manipulated (rotated, sized, moved) to meet specific needs.

Extensions of drawing programs are *computer-aided design (CAD)* applications. These sophisticated graphic packages facilitate the creation of precision line drawings and computer models used, for example, by aircraft designers or molecular biologists to simulate 3-dimensional objects.

Images created by these graphics programs can be printed on graphics printers. Many graphics programs also have the capability of outputting their images to the monitor in an automated slide show, one after another according to a pre-defined order and time schedule.

Desktop Publishers

Desktop publishing programs enable the combining of text created by a word processor and graphic images created by a graphics program for the purpose of producing documents such as newsletters, advertising flyers, or instruction manuals.

Many desktop publishers provide great flexibility in type styles and sizes for special-effect headlines or captions. They allow for flowing text around pictures, varying column widths, and creating fancy borders. Some of the more powerful word processing programs include some desktop publishing capability.

Communication Programs

Communication programs enable computers to connect to other personal computers or to mainframe computers for the purpose of sharing or exchanging information. Communication software is used in conjunction with a modem, a device that translates computer data to and from a format that can be transmitted over telephone lines.

Computer communications have varied uses. Writers working at home can transmit drafts to editors, locally or in other cities. Through communication with electronic bulletin board systems (BBS), users can access volumes of information to view airline schedules, find a specialized bibliography, or *download* (receive) a new computer game.

Electronic Mail

In addition to computer-to-computer communication that uses telephone lines, local area networks enable users to communicate with each other across network cables. Electronic mail programs allow users to type messages to each other, and even to send each other documents created by other applications. Combining telephone-line communications with electronic mail programs gives computer users easy, flexible, on-line access to other computer users all over the world.

Languages

A computer language is a program that enables the user to create other programs. No matter how many computer applications there are, there will always be a need for customized programming written especially to solve a specific problem.

A computer language, like a spoken language, has a vocabulary of words that can be used and a *syntax*, or set of grammar rules, that define how those words can be combined to create instructions. Programmers write *code* — lines of instructions — using the vocabulary and syntax of the language they have chosen to use. These languages include BASIC, Fortran, C, COBOL, and others.

When all the program code has been written, in a human-readable form, another part of the language package may be used to compile the program. Compilers translate typed lines of code into the electronic machine language that the CPU understands. Compiled programs are *executable* — they can be loaded into RAM and used to create and manipulate data.

Utilities and Environments

Utilities and Environments are add-ons. They generally are not used to create data, but they are used with other programs to provide additional features or to make the program easier to use.

Menu systems are utilities that make it easy to load programs or run commands by selecting them from a pre-defined menu of choices. There are utility programs that provide memory management capability — using available RAM to its best advantage. There are utilities that aid in diagnosing and solving problems with disks or lost data.

The Windows program is an environment which combines the features of a menu system with the capability of a memory management program, and more. In addition, Windows comes with its own included set of applications, including a word processor, a communications program, and others.

Operating Systems

Regardless of what you use your computer for, you must use an operating system. An operating system is a collection of programs that helps you to communicate with your computer and helps the various parts of the computer to communicate with each other.

The CPU merely reads and responds to instructions. It knows very little by itself. It must be told what to do when you press, for example, the W key on your keyboard. It must be told how to move data from RAM to a printer when you indicate you want to print, and how to store a document onto a disk when you indicate you want to save your data.

If each application program had to include these very basic instructions, the applications would be huge, cumbersome, and very expensive. Instead, these fundamental commands are taken care of by the operating system when the individual applications request them.

The operating system understands how to load programs into RAM. It is in charge of saving documents onto disks (and keeping track of exactly where each document is stored) and retrieving them back into RAM.

There are several operating systems. Each application program must be designed for the specific operating system under which it will be running. Each operating system handles basic operations such as printing, saving and retrieving data for every one of the applications used with it. Some of the more popular personal computer operating systems are DOS, OS/2, and UNIX.

Appendix
B

Installation and Setup

You have probably already gone through the Windows
setup process at least once when you first installed
Windows on your system. You may not remember, but the
program you used is called Setup, and it is a fairly easy
process. Windows Setup allows you to specify your
hardware configuration and set the environment in which
Windows will run.

After you have installed Windows, you can use Setup to
add new hardware that you have installed, to change
existing hardware configurations, or to add new
applications. In this section, you will learn about Windows
hardware configurations and how Setup works, both in its
initial operation and when used for maintenance.

This appendix will help you to:

*   Understand hardware configuration issues.

*   Use Setup to install Windows.

*   Install Windows and non-Windows applications.

*   Change your environment with Setup.

*   Modify Windows when you change hardware.

Hardware Configurations

Before installing Windows, there are some hardware
requirements that you should consider.

Processor and Memory Requirements

To install and use Windows 3.1 you must have at least an
80286 processor with 640 Kb of conventional memory and
256 Kb of extended memory. With this configuration
Windows will run in Standard mode.

If you have an 80386 processor (or better) with 640 Kb of conventional memory and 1024 Kb of extended memory, you will be able to run Windows in 386 Enhanced Mode.

For more information on memory and modes, see Appendix C.

Hard Disk Space

You should have at least 8MB to 10MB of free disk space for Windows to operate properly on a 80386 system and at least 6MB to 9MB on a 80286 system. Note that this is space to be used solely by Windows applications and files; it does not include space for data or other applications.

Floppy Drives

Today, most stand-alone systems have at least one floppy drive, and many have a high-density floppy drive. You need a floppy drive to transfer information and to load Windows. Windows is usually distributed on high-density diskettes, but you may order low-density ones from Microsoft if necessary.

Display Adapters/Monitors

You will need a display adapter and monitor that are supported by Windows. Windows supports many types of monitors. Drivers are included for CGA, EGA, VGA and Hercules adapters, among others.

Because Windows is a GUI environment, screen resolution can make a big difference in usability. For best results, you will probably want at least an EGA setup. Very good resolution is provided by 800 X 600 VGA or 1024 X 768 SuperVGA displays.

Input/Output Devices

Though you can use Windows with just a keyboard, you most likely will want to have a mouse (or some other type of pointing device) as well. A mouse will allow you to make more effective use of the interface.

Output can be to a printer, plotter, or other device. Just as it controls the interface, giving you a uniform environment for running applications, Windows also controls output, accessing output devices directly, rather than from each application.

Compatibility	Apart from minimum requirements and personal preferences, another hardware consideration is compatibility. Windows comes with a default set of drivers for a variety of hardware items. Included with the software is a Hardware Compatibility List which lists hardware that has been tested with Windows and certified to work. Before running Setup, you should look through the list. If your hardware is not completely compatible, you may have to choose special configurations during Setup to make Windows work properly.

Installing with Setup

You use the Windows Setup program to install Windows. Setup guides you through the process and:

- Determines what kind of hardware you have.

- Copies Windows files to your hard disk.

- Lets you select and configure a printer and/or install applications.

At the beginning of the installation, Windows searches for previous versions of Windows software on the hard disk. If it finds any, you are given a choice of either updating the previous version, or installing the new version in a different directory. When installation is complete, the Setup program is available as an icon in the Main program group. You can run Setup again when you add or change hardware, or when you want to change any of the options you first selected.

Express vs. Custom Setup	There are two methods you can use to setup Windows on your computer: Express Setup or Custom Setup.

The Express method is recommended because it lets the Windows program determine the hardware configuration and software applications on your system, simplifying the installation. Express Setup will automatically update any necessary files and build program item icons for software applications currently on the hard drive(s). The entire process consists of inserting the appropriate floppy disks |

when prompted. The only two technical items you must know are what kind of printer you are using and to which port it is connected (usually LPT1).

The Custom method should be used by experienced users who need to alter the normal configuration. This method will require you to answer questions about the type of computer, keyboard, mouse, and display you are using.

Running Setup the First Time

Windows software arrives on a set of disks. The Setup program is on Disk 1 of the set.

> **NOTE**: You cannot install Windows by copying the files from the Windows disks to your hard disk. The files are in a compressed format and are not usable until they have been expanded.

When you are ready to install Windows for the first time, follow this procedure:

1. Insert Disk 1 in your floppy drive and close the drive door.

2. Type the drive letter for the drive (**A:** or **B:**) and press **[Enter]**.

3. Type **setup** and press **[Enter]**.

After approximately 15 seconds, you will be prompted to select either Express or Custom setup. Press the **[Enter]** key for Express or the letter **c** for Custom.

Express Method

If you selected Express, from this point on follow the instructions on the screen. If you do not understand an instruction or option, press the F1 key for help.

During setup you will be asked to supply a name and company, which is required to continue setup. As the installation continues, a list box will display, prompting you for printer information. Use the scroll bar to find the correct printer and choose the Install button. You will also be asked to select the printer port from a list box. Printers are normally connected to LPT1.

Windows will then scan the hard disk(s) in order to build program-item icons. During this process you may be prompted to select the program names to be used.

When Setup has successfully completed, you will have to re-boot your computer. Then, to start Windows, type **win** and press **[Enter]**. When you do so, the Program Manager window, with the Main Group open, will appear on your screen.

Custom Method

If you selected Custom from the initial screen, Setup will ask for information, including: the directory for Windows files; the computer, monitor, mouse, and keyboard you are using; and your language. You may also have to: provide information about your network, select a printer and port, or choose applications to be installed.

When Setup has successfully completed, you will have to re-boot your computer. Then, to start Windows, type **win** and press **[Enter]**. When you do so, the Program Manager window, with the Main Group open, will appear on your screen.

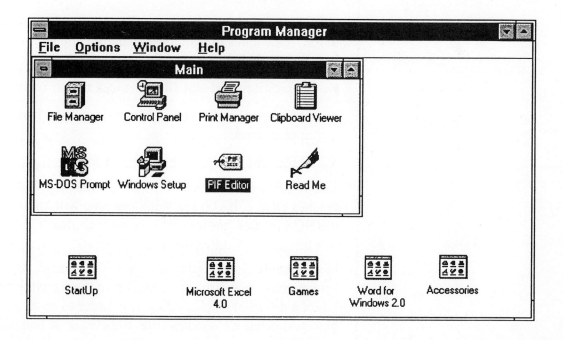

Setup /i Parameter

By default, Setup installs Windows on a stand-alone system and automatically detects the hardware in the system. You can change the operation of Setup with a command line parameter.

If you think Windows' detection of your hardware is causing a problem with Setup, you may want to try the /i parameter. If you use this switch, Setup will display the system configuration screen so you can choose the hardware items selectively. Before you do this, you will need to erase all the files in the Windows directory.

DOS and Windows Mode Setup

The Setup program has two modes: DOS mode and Windows mode. The first time you run Setup, you begin from DOS because that is the only available environment. In DOS mode, the Setup program:

- Asks for the default directory.

- Detects the hardware configuration.

- Copies the files necessary to run Windows.

- Loads Windows.

After Setup loads the minimum files required for Windows to run, it switches to Windows operation and completes the installation. In Windows mode, the Setup program:

- Copies standard and 386 enhanced files if required.

- Offers options for configuring printers and installing applications.

- Builds the groups in the Program Manager.

The Windows mode part of installation begins when Setup reaches Disk 2. If you see Windows, you will know that the DOS portion has installed the correct files.

A frequently encountered problem during installation is an incompatible display adapter. If Windows hangs, and the screen goes blank, try re-starting using the /i switch and select a different display adapter. In order to re-start Setup, you must delete all Windows files installed up to that point.

Installing Applications

Just as Setup can detect the hardware available on your system, it also searches for applications on your hard disk. If you have chosen Express Setup, Windows will search all drives and directories for programs. Although it will find all executable programs, it may prompt you to identify the specific program.

If you selected Custom Setup or used the /i switch, Setup will ask where to look for the files. After searching the specified drive(s), Setup presents a list of programs that it has found. Again, setup may not recognize all the programs on your disk, but will usually find the most common ones. You can choose which programs to add. If you like, you may add them all.

Windows Applications

If Setup finds Windows applications, it will create a program group called *Applications.* Then it will place the icon for each selected program in the group.

Non-Windows Applications and PIF Files

For non-Windows applications that it finds, Setup creates program icons and places them in the *Applications* program group. Setup will also construct a PIF file for executing each application.

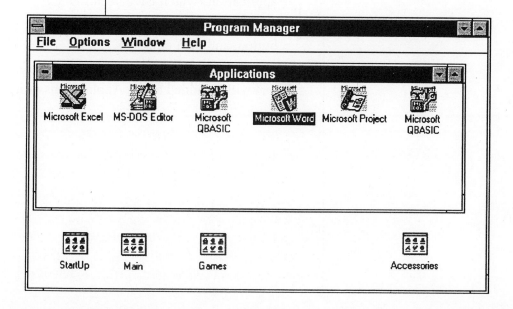

Using Setup for Maintenance

After the initial installation, you can use Setup from within Windows or from the DOS prompt to make changes to your setup. Which mode you use will depend on the type of changes you are making. If you need to verify the system configuration chosen by Windows or to add or change a device driver that is not part of the Windows default set, then you must run Setup from the DOS prompt.

On the other hand, if you are making minor adjustments like changing mouse drivers from one default driver to another, you will probably find it easier to use Setup from within Windows. Similarly, Windows mode Setup provides an easy way to install a new application.

Adding an Application

After you have installed Windows, you can use Setup to add applications at any time. To do so, follow this procedure:

1. Start the Windows Setup program.

2. Select the **Options** menu and choose **Set Up Applications**.

3. Select the drives to be searched.

4. When Windows has finished searching, examine the applications which have been found.

5. Select the application name(s) in the list; click the **Add** button, and then click **OK**.

The program-item icons for the applications you have selected will be added to the Applications program group.

Changing Device Drivers

If you want to change from one supported device to another, you can start Setup from within Windows. To do so, follow this procedure:

1. Start the Windows Setup program.

2. Open the Options menu and choose Change System Settings. The Change System Settings dialog box is displayed.

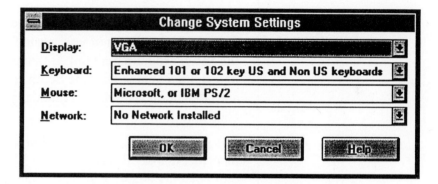

3. Choose the item you wish to change and use the drop-down list to select the new driver from the available choices.

4. After making changes, click OK. Then re-start Windows.

    Note: Even though it is possible to change the display adapter from Windows mode Setup, doing so is not recommended. Because the display adapter is one of the most critical settings, you should start Setup from DOS mode for this type of change.

Changing Device Drivers DOS Mode

Some hardware devices have special drivers that are not part of the Windows default set. For devices of this type, you must supply the driver. The driver will usually be available from the device manufacturer. To add a non-supported device driver you must start Setup from DOS. To do so:

1. From the Windows directory, type:

    setup and press [Enter]

If you do not start from the Windows directory, Setup will assume that you are trying to install a new version.

2. Select the setting you want to change and follow the instructions on the screen. One of the driver choices will be Other. When you select this, Setup will prompt you for the disk containing the driver files.

3. Insert the disk and continue to follow on-screen instructions to complete installation of the driver file.

Setup Problems

The initial part of Setup uses an auto-detection program to analyze the hardware of your system. During this phase, the Setup program may fail. If this occurs, you may want to use the /i switch with the Setup command. This disables auto-detection and lets you manually select the hardware configuration.

The primary cause of program failure during Setup is an incorrect display driver selection. Usually this occurs with older display adapters. If this should occur, you may try selecting a more generic adapter during Setup, such as EGA or VGA. If this also fails, you may have to contact your display manufacturer to supply the appropriate driver.

Appendix
C

Optimizing Windows

By now, you should be familiar with the graphical user interface and multitasking of application programs that Windows provides. After you have been working with Windows for a while, you may want to look at ways in which you can optimize your installation and usage to improve performance. You will have the best results if you focus on two main areas: memory and disk space.

This appendix will help you to:

- Understand the types of memory available on your computer.

- Describe how Windows uses memory.

- Understand the operating modes of Windows.

- Understand temporary and permanent swap files.

- Create a permanent swap file.

- Set up disk caching.

Memory Overview

Understanding random access memory (RAM) is very important for understanding Windows 3.1 operation. The RAM of your computer is a temporary storage medium for programs and data. When you want to work with a program, it must be loaded into memory in order to run. Simply put, the more RAM your system has available, the faster these applications will run. When you are finished, the program and data can be stored on a permanent storage device like a hard drive.

There are three types of memory which may be available on your personal computer:

- Conventional memory

- Expanded memory

- Extended memory

Additionally, Windows uses a fourth type of memory called virtual memory, which is discussed later.

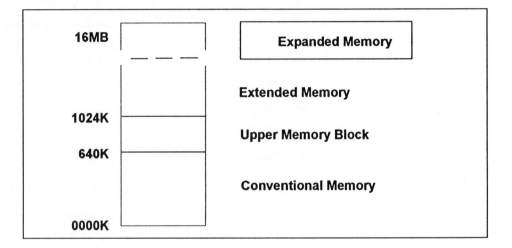

Conventional Memory

All personal computers have *conventional memory*. Conventional memory is the first 640K bytes of RAM that is available on your system. The operating system (DOS) and any utilities and applications found in your CONFIG.SYS and AUTOEXEC.BAT files use this memory. When you start your machine, it runs through some checks and loads these into memory. Any remaining memory is available for running other applications.

Until recently, 640K was the maximum addressable memory. This limited both the size of applications which could be run and the speed with which they ran. With newer processors and Windows 3.1, this restriction has been overcome.

The Upper Memory Block

The *upper memory block (UMB)* is the memory between 640K and 1024k. It is sometimes referred to as the *adapter segment* because it is the area of memory used by hardware adapters, for example, the display adapter or a network card. The UMB is also the area in which an expanded memory manager makes memory available to applications requiring it.

Expanded Memory

Expanded memory is additional memory from an add-on memory board or a memory emulator that you install on your system. Expanded memory allows you to run DOS applications that are larger or to run applications faster. An expanded memory manager is required to access expanded memory. Expanded memory is used in this way:

• A program requests more memory than is available in conventional memory.

• The expanded memory manager gets the memory from the expanded memory board and makes it available to the program.

• The memory is made available in a *page frame* in the UMB. Information from the expanded memory is not actually copied into memory; its addresses are mapped.

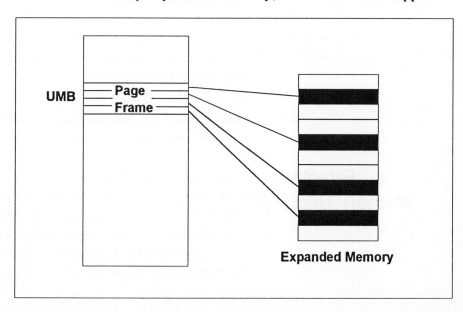

UMB   Page Frame

Expanded Memory

Expanded memory was an attempt to get past the 640K restriction on conventional memory, and in so doing, to allow larger and faster applications. Several companies in the industry, including Lotus, Intel, and Microsoft cooperated to define standards for the operation of expanded memory. The standard is known as LIM EMS (for Lotus-Intel-Microsoft Expanded Memory Specification). Many non-Windows applications use expanded memory.

Expanded memory has several disadvantages: it requires special hardware and software, applications must be re-written to use it, and it is slower than other types of memory.

Extended Memory

Extended memory is so called because it is an extension of the original 1 megabyte of RAM that is available on 80286 and 80386 processors. Extended memory is a *seamless* continuation of memory which begins at address 1024K where the upper memory block ends. An operating system that can access more than 1M of memory can address extended memory in a linear fashion as though it were conventional memory. Memory then appears as one contiguous block.

DOS, however, can only address 1M of memory (640K conventional and the UMB). To add an extended memory addressing capability to DOS requires an *extended memory manager*. Windows has its own extended memory manager called HIMEM.SYS.

Extended memory, because it can be accessed as a contiguous block, provides better performance than expanded memory.

Effective Memory Usage

Probably the biggest single thing you can do to enhance Windows performance is to add extended memory to your system. You can add memory by purchasing additional RAM for installation on your system mother board or by purchasing an extended memory board which you install in an expansion slot. Be sure that the RAM is extended, not expanded, memory.

If you add extended memory, be sure that Windows has installed the extended memory manager HIMEM.SYS. There should be a command in your CONFIG.SYS file to load HIMEM.SYS or a compatible extended memory manager.

Making the Most of Expanded Memory

Windows does not directly access expanded memory. In Standard mode, expanded memory is available to DOS applications through an external expanded memory manager. In 386 Enhanced mode, Windows uses extended memory to simulate expanded memory.

Some expanded memory boards can be re-configured as extended memory, which Windows can access. If you have this type of board, check the documentation that came with it for instructions on how to re-configure it. Some boards accomplish this through software; for others, you will have to set switches on the board.

If your board cannot be used as extended memory, you may want to explore using some of the expanded memory for disk caching as described later in this section.

Conserving Memory at Startup

When you start up your computer, two files define your hardware environment and what gets loaded into memory. These files are CONFIG.SYS and AUTOEXEC.BAT. Any programs, drivers, or utilities that are contained in these files are loaded into memory when you turn on your machine.

Your AUTOEXEC.BAT file may load terminate-and-stay-resident programs (TSRs) when the system boots. These are programs which are loaded into memory and are executed by a special keystroke combination. They can take up a lot of memory that would otherwise be available for Windows.

You can save or free up additional memory prior to starting Windows by eliminating any unnecessary drivers from the DOS startup files. For example, if you only use a mouse in Windows and Windows applications, you do not need to load the mouse driver in CONFIG.SYS or AUTOEXEC.BAT. Windows uses its own mouse driver. Be careful, though, about removing drivers. Some, like network drivers, must be loaded before you start Windows; others, like HIMEM.SYS, are required by Windows itself.

Additional memory savings can be gained by removing any TSRs from the AUTOEXEC.BAT file. Since Windows treats TSRs like any other DOS application, it is best to start them when you need them from within Windows. You can then switch to them whenever you like.

Loading unnecessary drivers and TSRs is particularly ineffective if you run Windows in 386 Enhanced mode. In 386 Enhanced mode, Windows creates a virtual machine for each DOS application. Any drivers or TSRs that you load at startup are then duplicated in every virtual machine.

You can make changes to the CONFIG.SYS and AUTOEXEC.BAT files using any ASCII text editor, including the Windows Notepad accessory. For more information on changing these files, refer to the *Microsoft Windows User's Guide*.

> **Caution:** Before you modify either file, make a bootable disk and copy both files onto it. In this way, you will be able to boot from the floppy if there is any problem.

Memory Savings in Windows

To check how much memory is available when you are working in Windows, pull down the **Help** menu in the Program Manager and select **About Program Manager.**

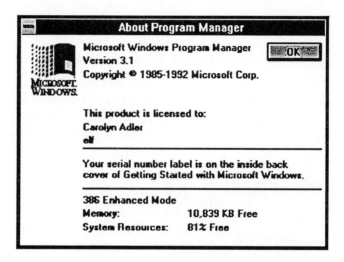

The amount of free memory is shown in K bytes. If you are running in 386 Enhanced mode, the number may be greater than the amount of physical memory in the machine. In 386 Enhanced mode, Windows uses virtual memory management to make more RAM available to applications. Virtual memory is discussed later in this section.

System Resources

You will also see the percentage of *system resources* that are free. The system resources percentage and the amount of free memory are unrelated.

To understand system resources, you need to understand a little about Windows internal architecture. There are three major components in the Windows core: Kernel, Graphics Device Interface (GDI), and User.

GDI and User have their own storage areas, called heaps, that are limited in size. The GDI heap is local and is 64 Kb; User has two heaps of 64 Kb each. Every window and icon that is created uses this space. The percentage of free system resources is the remaining combined GDI and User space.

Here are some things you can do while working in Windows to conserve memory and system resources:

1.   When you are finished with an application, close it.

2.   Run DOS applications full-screen rather than windowed.

3.   Minimize any Windows applications you are not using.

4.   Do not use wallpaper on your desktop.

Note: It is possible to receive an Out of Memory error message even with a large amount of free memory. If this happens, check the system resources, and, if you are low, try some of the above steps to resolve the problem.

What Does Windows Require?

You can run Windows 3.1 on 80286 or faster machines with MS-DOS version 3.1 or later. For optimal performance, it is recommended that you upgrade to MS-DOS version 5.0 because of its more efficient memory management capabilities. Windows operates in one of two modes based on the available memory, as shown in the following table:

Processor	Memory	Mode
80286	640 Kb conventional + 256 Kb extended	Standard
80386 or better	640 Kb conventional + 256 Kb extended	Standard
80386 or better	640 Kb conventional + 1024 Kb extended	386 Enhanced

When it starts, Windows automatically determines how much memory is available and in which mode to operate. In general, the more extended memory you have, the better Windows will run.

Operating Modes

As you have seen, Windows 3.1 operates in either Standard or 386 Enhanced mode. When it starts, Windows automatically chooses the mode in which it will operate based on your processor and available memory.

The two operating modes interact with the available types of memory in different ways, and each mode has advantages and disadvantages.

If necessary, you can start Windows in a mode other than the default. To force Windows to start in a different mode, you use a parameter on the startup command line.

Type:	To start:
win /s	Standard mode
win /3	386 Enhanced mode

Standard Mode

Standard mode is the normal mode for running Windows 3.1 on 80286 processors. In this mode, Windows can access extended memory, breaking the 640 Kb conventional barrier. In Standard mode, Windows does not use expanded memory. Expanded memory can be available for DOS applications using an external expanded memory manager. Any non-Windows applications that use extended memory will run in Standard mode. Consider the following before selecting Standard mode:

- **Configuration:**

  You are using an 80286 or better computer.

  You have at least 640K of conventional memory and 256K of extended.

- **When to Use:**

  You want to run only Windows applications and have plenty of extended memory.

  You are troubleshooting enhanced mode problems.

- **Advantages:**

  Can be up to 20% faster than enhanced mode.

  Makes use of extended memory, allowing larger programs to run.

  Provides multitasking for Windows applications.

- **Disadvantages:**

  Does not allow multitasking for non-Windows applications.

  Is limited to the amount of memory that is physically available.

Standard mode may be the best choice if you are running exclusively Windows applications. It has effective memory management and provides fast performance in that environment.

386 Enhanced Mode

Like Standard mode, 386 Enhanced mode makes use of all available conventional and extended memory. Similarly, 386 Enhanced mode does not use expanded memory. For applications which require expanded memory, 386 Enhanced mode makes extended memory look like expanded memory to the application.

Additionally, 386 Enhanced mode uses the 80386's virtual mode to segment extended memory into conventional memory blocks. In this way, each DOS application can run in its own virtual machine. Each virtual machine has a copy of the operating system and drivers. Windows and Windows applications run in another virtual machine.

386 Enhanced mode also makes use of *virtual memory*. In this mode, Windows simulates memory using the hard drive. To do so, it creates a *swap file* on your disk and treats it like extended memory, swapping information to and from memory and the hard disk. Consider the following before selecting 386 Enhanced mode:

- **Configuration:**

  You are using an 80386 or better computer.

  You have 640K of conventional memory and 1024K of extended memory.

- **When to Use:**

  You run multiple non-Windows applications concurrently.

  You need more memory than is physically available.

- **Advantages:**

  Multitasking for both Windows and non-Windows applications.

  Simulates more memory than is actually present.

- **Disadvantages:**

  Can be slower than Standard mode.

  Is the most complex mode.

386 Enhanced mode is the most powerful mode of Windows operation and provides the best performance when you are mixing Windows and non-Windows applications.

Managing Your Hard Drive

Next to memory, an area where you can look for possible performance enhancements is your hard disk drive. The hard disk is generally where you store the operating system and application programs, as well as your data or document files. As application programs have become increasingly large and complex, they require more hard disk space.

Windows uses the hard disk for storing applications and files and also for swapping information in and out of memory. This means that the amount of free disk space you have can impact on multitasking in Windows. It can also affect the speed with which Windows operates.

A few areas that can increase performance of Windows are:

- The amount of free disk space available
- Disk compacting
- Use of swap files
- Disk caching

These are discussed in the remainder of this section.

Good Disk Habits

Because hard disk space is a valuable commodity in the Windows environment, you should take steps to manage the space most effectively. Good hard disk management habits include:

- Organize your disk into directories and subdirectories.
- Keep programs and data in separate directories.
- Backup your data files regularly.
- Delete unnecessary files.

Compacting Your Hard Disk

Even if you do all of these things, you cannot control where the operating system stores files on the disk and whether files are stored in contiguous sectors or are scattered around on the disk. Over time, your files can become fragmented. When this happens, the disk is cluttered and access is slower.

You can use a utility program called a de-fragmentation or disk compacting utility to relocate files and make available more space in contiguous sectors. When you use one of these programs, fragmented files are brought together and contiguous free space is created at the end of the disk. This results in more space and faster access.

Compacting your hard disk is particularly important if you want to create a permanent swap file as described below.

Swap Files

Besides storing programs and data, Windows uses hard disk space to swap information from memory to disk and back to memory. Swapping is handled differently depending on the mode in which you are running.

Swapping in Standard Mode

In Standard mode, Windows creates a temporary *application* swap file for each DOS application you start as well as one for the Windows environment. This is how multitasking in this mode is accomplished. If you are working in Windows and execute a DOS application, the Windows task is swapped from memory to disk, and the DOS application is swapped into memory. The reverse happens when you switch back to Windows from the DOS application. The files that are created are called *application swap files*. They are temporary and are deleted when the DOS application is terminated.

Windows stores the application swap files in one of three places:

- In **the drive and directory specified by the swapdisk=** setting in the SYSTEM.INI file. You can edit the SYSTEM.INI file to include a swap drive and directory using either the Windows Notepad or Sysedit.

- If no swapdisk has been specified, Windows stores them in **the drive and directory specified in the environment variable TEMP**. The Windows Setup program normally sets up this TEMP variable. You can specify the location by including a TEMP statement in your AUTOEXEC.BAT file. For example, the statement TEMP=C:\TEMP will cause temporary files to be stored in the TEMP directory of the C: drive.

- If no TEMP variable is specified, Windows will place the files in **the root directory of the first hard disk**.

The names of application swap files begin with the characters ~WOA. The files are erased when you quit the DOS application.

Swapping in 386 Enhanced Mode

In 386 Enhanced mode, Windows handles disk swapping differently. Instead of creating individual application swap files for each application, Windows uses a single swap file.

Then, if it is low on memory, Windows swaps the contents of memory out to this file.

During Windows Setup, the program will attempt to create a permanent swap file based on the amount of free disk space. If it cannot, Windows will automatically create a temporary swap file whenever you start in 386 Enhanced mode.

If an applications tries to locate information in memory that has been swapped to the disk, the Virtual Memory Manager reloads the requested information from disk into memory.

Temporary Swap Files

If it finds no permanent swap file when it starts in 386 Enhanced mode, Windows creates a temporary swap file called WIN386.SWP. Windows sizes the temporary swap file dynamically according to its requirements and deletes the file automatically when you exit. By default, the file is stored in the Windows directory.

> **Note:** You must have at least 1.5M of free disk space if you want Windows to have virtual memory support through a temporary swap file.

Creating a Permanent Swap File

If you run in 386 Enhanced mode and use many DOS applications, creating a permanent swap file is a good way to improve performance. When you create a permanent swap file, you are setting aside a contiguous area of the hard disk to use for disk swapping. The file that you create remains on disk even when you are not using Windows.

A permanent swap file actually is composed of two files. The first is a hidden file named 386SPART.PAR that is located in the root directory of the hard drive. The second file is a read-only file named SPART.PAR stored in the Windows directory.

> **Caution:** Do NOT delete, move, or attempt to modify these files other than through the Control Panel 386 Enhanced dialog box.

Before creating a swap file, you will probably want to compact your disk as described earlier. In this way, you will free up the maximum contiguous space on the disk.

Pros and Cons

A permanent swap file is only used if you run Windows in 386 Enhanced mode. You should consider creating one if you run many DOS applications from Windows or if you run large applications which require more memory than your machine has.

The major advantage of a permanent swap file over a temporary one is speed of access. This is because a permanent swap file is in a contiguous area of the disk while the temporary swap file may be in fragments.

The primary disadvantage is the loss of disk space. Unlike the temporary swap file, which is deleted when you exit Windows, the permanent file remains on disk. The space it uses is unavailable even when you are not running Windows.

Creating Swap Files for Virtual Memory

You can create a swap file during Setup or choose the Control Panel 386 Enhanced icon to either create or modify temporary and permanent swap files.

1.   Select the Control Panel from the Main program group.

2.   Select the 386 Enhanced sub-program.

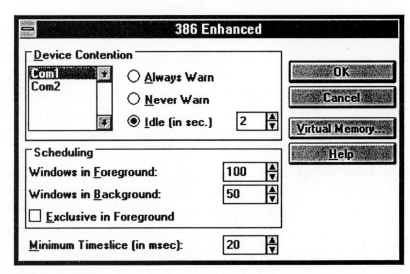

3.   Choose the Virtual Memory button, and then the Change button.

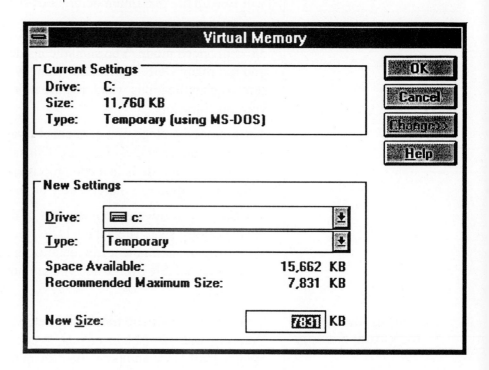

4.   Make any changes that you require: choose a drive letter; choose the type of swap file (permanent, temporary, or none) and click OK.

5.   Re-start Windows so that your changes will take effect.

Windows may recommend a swap file size as large as half of the available disk space. You can change the size if desired. As a rule of thumb, you should allocate as much disk space (if there is enough) for the swap file as there is memory in your machine.

Disk Caching

No matter how much you optimize hard disk space and your usage of it, accessing the hard disk will usually be slower than accessing memory. Each time you want to use information from the disk, the system accesses the disk and reads the information into memory.

What Is Disk Caching?

You can improve disk retrieval performance by utilizing a technique known as *disk caching*. This technique reserves a portion of memory, known as a cache, for information accessed from a disk. Then, the next time the information is required, it is accessed from the memory cache instead of from the disk. Similarly, information to be written to the disk is stored temporarily in the cache and written when resources are in less demand.

Windows comes with a disk caching utility called SMARTDrive, which it installs by default during Setup if your system has enough memory. Setup configures SMARTDrive with a cache size based on the amount of RAM installed on your system.

You can check to see if SMARTDrive is installed by looking in your CONFIG.SYS or AUTOEXEC.BAT file. If you do not find a command for SMARTDrive, you may have to install it. To do so, add a line to your CONFIG.SYS file like:

    device=c:\windows\smartdrv.sys 1024 512

This causes the system to look for the driver in the Windows directory and install it so that the initial cache size is 1024 Kb and the Windows cache size is 512 Kb. The initial size is the size of the cache before Windows runs. The Windows cache size is the amount that Windows can reduce the cache size.

With a larger cache size, your system accesses the disk drive less often, and performance is improved. Setup configures the default disk cache based on available extended memory according to the following table:

Extended Memory	Initial Cache Size	Windows Cache Size
Up to 1 M	All extended memory	Zero (no caching)
Up to 2M	1M	256K
Up to 4M	1M	512K
Up to 6M	2M	1M
6M or more	2M	2M

In addition to controlling the size, you can specify other parameters for SMARTDrive. For additional information, refer to the *Microsoft Windows User's Guide*.

Note: If you modify CONFIG.SYS to install SMARTDrive, be sure to put the SMARTDrive command after the extended memory manager driver.

Appendix
D

Windows and Networks

By now, you should be comfortable with most aspects of Windows installation and operation on a single-user PC. This appendix provides information about Windows installation and use in multi-user environments on a network.

This appendix will help you to:

- Recognize sources of technical information on Windows and networks.

- Know how to set up Windows on a network server.

- Know how to set up Windows on workstations.

- Understand the use of network resources.

- Be aware of ways to optimize a network.

About Networks

There are many different types of *Local Area Networks (LANs)* and network software. Though they are different in specifics, most LANs are operationally similar. This section provides a very brief introduction to general network terminology. In practice, you should be quite familiar with the specifics of how your network operates before attempting to install Windows for network use.

Networks are designed to allow users to: share programs and data, access shared resources like disk space and printers, and communicate with one another. Computers that are connected to a network are sometimes called *workstations*. Each workstation communicates with the network through a *network card*. Networks usually have at least one computer which acts as a *server*. The server may have added hardware and software, and it controls access to the shared resources of the network.

Workstation users log on to the network when they want to use common files or need network resources. Log on establishes communication between the workstation and the network. Access to files or resources is normally controlled through a system of user privileges maintained by an administrator.

Supported Networks

Some application programs are written for use on single-user PCs only. Others are designed to work exclusively on networks. Still others have both single-user and network versions. Windows can be both a single-user application or a networked one.

Microsoft has worked with various network vendors to test the ability of Windows to operate reliably on their networks. Those in which the tests have been successful are referred to as *supported* networks. Other networks, where successful testing has not been accomplished, are *unsupported*. The lists of supported and unsupported networks are constantly changing. It is best to check with the vendor to know whether its network is compatible with Windows.

More Information

For details of installing and running Windows on specific networks, request the Windows *Resource Kit* manual from Microsoft Technical Support. You may also find useful information in the NETWORKS.WRI file that comes with Windows. To view this document, use the Write accessory program.

Network Installations

You can choose to install Windows on a network server or on a workstation. If you install on a workstation which has a hard drive, you can choose whether to run Windows from a directory on the server or from the local hard drive. Of course, for a workstation which does not have a hard drive, you must run Windows from the server.

If you choose to install Windows on each workstation, it will require 8M to 11M of hard disk space on each workstation. If you choose to install a shared copy of windows on the server, you will require 16M of disk space on the file server and 300K on each workstation.

Network Server Administrative Installation

Regardless of how you want to set up Windows on a network, you must place the required Windows files on the server. Windows makes this process very simple by adding a switch to the normal Setup command.

Do NOT attempt to copy the files to the server without using Setup. These files are compressed files that must be expanded and renamed in order for Windows to be installed properly. In addition, the Setup program will automatically make the files read-only. This is necessary so that multiple users and applications can access the same files.

When you are ready to begin installation, log on to the network server. You will need a high level of access (e.g., administrator) because you will be creating read-only directories and files. After you have logged on, follow the steps below to install Windows on a network server.

1.   Log on to the network server.

2.   Insert the Windows Setup disk 1 in the floppy drive.

3.   Change to the floppy drive by typing **A:** and pressing **[Enter]**.

4.   Type *setup /a*.

5.   Follow the instructions on the screen.

During the Administrative Installation of Windows, you will be prompted to supply the drive and directory where you want to copy the files.

Once you complete installation on the server, you will then be able to install windows on the workstations. The Administrative installation does not set up a working copy of Windows. It is intended only to place the necessary files on the server so that individual workstations can run Windows.

If you look at the files in the directory, you will notice that there are no initialization files (neither WIN.INI nor SYSTEM.INI). This is because Windows is not run from the network installation directory, but from a user directory. You must run Setup with the /n parameter from a workstation before Windows can execute.

Workstation Installation

You install a shared version of Windows on workstations in the network by running Setup with the /n parameter. Setup will ask for a location for the individual user's Windows files. You can choose to load these files either on the workstation's hard drive or in a user directory on the network server.

Before you install Windows on a workstation, you should decide which location is best for your configuration and how you plan to operate. Workstation installation is accomplished by connecting to the network drive and directory that contains the Windows files. The floppy disks are not used.

To install Windows on a network workstation, use the following steps:

1. Connect to the Network server and drive that contains the Windows files.

2. At the command prompt type *setup /n*.

3. Follow the instructions on the screen to install Windows on the workstation's hard drive or the file server. The two choices are described below.

Workstation Hard Drive

If the local workstation is equipped with a large hard drive and you want to allow more individual control of Windows, install the user files on the hard drive. This type of installation minimizes network traffic and encourages personalized configurations, but makes upgrades and backups more difficult.

User Directory on Server

If the local workstations have small hard drives and/or you want more central control of the Windows configuration, install the individual user files in a user directory on the server. This installation minimizes the use of the local hard drive and provides for easier centralized administration. It may, however, result in network performance problems, as well as taking down users when the server is down.

Diskless Workstation

If the local workstations have no hard drives at all, you must install the individual user files in a personal user directory on the server. This installation provides maximum security and centralized control, but introduces high network traffic.

To complete workstation installation, you may need to modify your boot configuration to accommodate Windows. If you install on a server directory, Setup will create sample files called AUTOEXEC.WIN and CONFIG.WIN which you can use as models.

Lastly, check to be sure that the path statement in the AUTOEXEC.BAT file includes the directory on the server containing the server Windows installation and the user directory containing the individual user files. The user directory should be first in the path.

Working on a Network

Once installation is complete, you should be able to use network resources from within Windows. There are a few things you should keep in mind when beginning to work on a network.

- Always start the network before running Windows.

- Unless your network supports a Windows log in function, log in before running Windows.

- If your network supports Windows log in, log in via the Network section of the Control Panel. Do not log in to the network from a DOS command window.

After you have started the network and logged on, type **win** and press **[Enter]**. Windows starts to run in the mode determined by your workstation's processor and memory.

Connecting Network Drives

In order to access programs and data files which are on the server, you must connect the server directories to local drive identifiers. You use File Manager to associate a local drive letter with a directory on the network server.

If network drives have already been associated before you start Windows, you will see network drive icons in the File Manager menu bar. To use File Manager to connect a network drive, select the **Disk, Network Connections** command. This allows you to choose a drive letter and enter a network server directory path to be associated with it.

To connect to a network drive, do the following:

1. Choose **File Manager** from the Main program group.
2. Select **Disk, Network Connections**.
3. Use the Dialog box to select the path and drive designators you want connected.
4. If required, fill in the password text box.
5. Click the **Connect** button.
6. Make any additional connections.
7. When finished, choose the **Close** button.

Once you have connected to a network drive, you will see a drive icon that represents the association. From then on, you can access the network drive just as you would a local drive. This includes starting programs which reside on the drive and reading and writing data files. Note that you must have the necessary permissions or privileges for the directory on the server.

Each time you start Windows, these connections will be made. You can make additional connections as well as disconnections by following the previous steps. If you want to disconnect from a network drive, choose the **Disconnect** button instead of the **Connect** button.

Printing

Printing to a network printer is not much more complicated than printing to a local one. You can connect a network printer by using the Network button from the Printers section of the Control Panel. Select the network printer that you wish to connect and select a port to which it will be logically connected. Before you print to the network printer, make sure that the printer driver for that printer is assigned to the port you have selected, and that the driver is active.

When you work on a single-user PC, Windows uses Print Manager to spool print jobs and control the print queue. When you print to a network printer, Windows bypasses Print Manager by default. This is because most networks incorporate their own print spooler and queue control. You can still use Print Manager to view the network queue. If you do so, you will see all the print jobs that are pending for the selected printer.

Optimizing

Just as on a single-user system, RAM and disk space are the keys to optimizing Windows performance on a network. For improved performance from the network server:

- Make sure the server has plenty of RAM and hard disk space.

- De-fragment the server disk frequently.

- Make sure that the server is not overloaded.

On the workstation, the network shell software may use a large portion of conventional memory. If you are only running Windows applications, this is not a problem because they can use extended memory. Still, the amount of RAM available to DOS applications will be limited. You can improve this situation, if you:

- Use a network shell that can be loaded into expanded or extended memory.

- Load network drivers into the UMB with an external memory manager.

Remember that Windows uses disk space for swap files. Swap to a local hard drive if your workstation has one that is large enough, and try to avoid swapping over the network.

Appendix
E

Troubleshooting

You have seen ways to make Windows and your system perform at their best, but what happens when things go wrong? It's then time for troubleshooting.

Troubleshooting means identifying a problem and implementing a solution. This appendix describes a general procedure for troubleshooting in the Windows environment. You will also look at some commonly encountered problems and ways to solve them.

This appendix will help you to:

- Know the general steps to take to identify a problem.

- Understand the different types of problems that may occur.

- Be aware of commonly encountered problems and their solutions.

- Solve setup and operational problems.

Problem-Solving Procedure

If you have trouble installing Windows or making it operate as you expect, you should use a procedure for finding out why. The first step after a problem occurs is trying to reproduce the problem under various circumstances. Some steps to take are:

1. **Minimize your configuration.**

   To minimize your configuration, remove all unnecessary drivers, TSRs, and other programs from your CONFIG.SYS and AUTOEXEC.BAT files. Only keep the minimum required to run your computer and to start Windows in Standard Mode.

Before you modify either of these files, it is wise to make backup copies of them on a system disk. That way, if something goes wrong, you'll be able to recover. Remember, too, that you must re-boot your system to see the effect of modifications to these startup files.

2.   **Start Windows in a different operating mode.**

You can isolate the problem area by trying to run Windows in a different operating mode. If you are having problems running Windows in 386 Enhanced mode, try running in Standard (win /s).

As you will see in just a bit, there are different problems related to the different modes, as well as different specific steps to take in solving them.

3.   **Use the README and other WRI files.**

These files are supplied on the Windows disks and contain useful and timely information regarding hardware configurations, drivers, etc. The information they contain may alert you to potential problems or help you to choose the right Setup options.

4.   **Get technical help.**

When you have exhausted your own resources, seek assistance either from Windows experts in your own organization or from Microsoft Technical Support. Before you call, make sure that you know basic information about your hardware and software configuration and that you can describe what you were trying to do and what happened.

In the rest of this appendix, you will find tips for troubleshooting problems in two categories: Setup failure and operational problems.

Setup Problems

Prior to its release, Windows was tested on thousands of computers and configurations. This does not necessarily mean, however, that your particular configuration was tested. You may have older or newer hardware which is not recognized by Setup and which causes problems.

DOS Mode Failure

Windows Setup runs first in DOS mode and then in Windows mode. The DOS portion of Setup detects the hardware configuration and then loads all the necessary files for Windows.

Problem:

Setup hangs before you see the screen which lists the hardware it has detected. The auto detection sequence may not be working properly.

Solution:

You can turn off auto detection by starting Setup with the /i parameter. From the DOS prompt,, type: **setup /i** and press **[Enter]**. Setup will not try to determine the hardware, but will select a standard default configuration. Note that unless your hardware matches the default, you will have to change the settings manually.

Windows Mode Problems

If the DOS portion of Setup completes successfully and the Windows portion begins, then Setup asks for Disk 2. The Windows portion of Setup installs the Windows applications and files and sets up groups.

Problem:

The system hangs and/or the screen goes blank. The majority of problems when Setup fails at this point are due to an incorrect display adapter. If you have an older machine or display adapter, it may not be correctly identified.

Solution:

Some older display adapters may not be identified correctly during auto detection. Re-run Setup with the /i parameter and select another display adapter when the hardware configuration screen appears.

Problem:

A Setup failure caused by insufficient memory.

Solution:

Remove any unnecessary device drivers and TSRs from your CONFIG.SYS and AUTOEXEC.BAT files. Re-boot and try Setup again.

Problem:

You do not have enough disk space to install Windows.

Solution:

Instead of using Express Setup, choose Custom Setup. This gives you control of how much Windows software gets installed. As you select/delete the items from the menu, the disk space usage is displayed at the bottom of the Dialog box. The only other solution is to scan the contents of the disk for files that you can delete. In particular, look for large graphics files that you do not need.

Problem:

Mouse action is jumpy or erratic in the Windows portion of Setup.

Solution:

Make sure that your mouse is compatible and that you are using the latest version of the mouse driver.

When you have successfully completed Setup, you should, at a minimum, be able to run Windows in Standard mode. Remember, though, that if your configuration changes, you will have to run Setup again to ensure proper operation.

Operational Problems

Once you have set up and installed Windows, you may experience difficulties in trying to start Windows in a particular mode or while working with it. If Windows doesn't start or run as you expect it to, you may have to run Setup again or modify your DOS and Windows startup files.

Problem:

Windows programs are slower than normal.

Solution:

There are a number of solutions. The hard disk may be nearly full or fragmented, which affects the performance of Windows. Try deleting those files/programs you do not need. You may also want to de-fragment your disk using one of the many third party utility programs. The last solution is to add more memory to your system, which can significantly improve performance.

Problem:

The mouse does not work.

Solution:

Make sure that your mouse is connected to either COM1 or COM2. If it is physically connected, then use Windows Setup to see if the mouse is correctly identified. If you installed the mouse after you installed Windows, you will have to use Setup to add the mouse to the hardware configuration.

Standard Mode

If you were able to successfully complete Setup, you should be able to run Windows in Standard mode. If your machine won't start in Standard mode, there are several possible problems.

Problem:

Your hardware configuration has changed, but the drivers are still the same.

Solution:

Run Windows Setup from within Windows to select the new driver(s). Setup will copy the driver files and revise the SYSTEM.INI file.

Problem:

A file that Windows needs (e.g., WIN.COM) has been corrupted or deleted.

Solution:

Make sure that all necessary files are on your system. Remember that you cannot simply copy files from the Windows installation disks because they are in compressed format.

Problem:

Your hardware has not changed, all files are intact, but Windows still won't start.

Solution:

Check to see whether you have enough conventional memory to start Windows. If you have loaded a TSR, there may not be enough memory left to start Windows. Re-boot and try again without the TSR.

Problem:

You do not have an extended memory manager loaded.

Solution:

Check to see that HIMEM.SYS or a compatible memory manager is loaded in your CONFIG.SYS file.

Problem:

You have an extended memory manager loaded, but Windows still won't start in Standard mode.

Solution:

Make sure that you are using the latest version of HIMEM.SYS and that you have enough memory to load it. Also, make sure that HIMEM.SYS is loaded by

CONFIG.SYS before any other device drivers that use extended memory.

386 Enhanced Mode

If you can run in Standard mode but not 386 Enhanced mode, the problem is probably one of Upper Memory Block (UMB) contention. The UMB is the memory between 640K and 1M that is typically used for adapters. A contention arises when 386 Enhanced mode tries to access a segment of the UMB that is already being used; this usually causes Windows to hang.

In 386 Enhanced mode, Windows must switch to 8086/8088 mode to write to disk or network devices. Because that mode only supports memory addressing up to 1M, Windows must place data, referred to as *translation buffers*, in that range. If it finds space in UMB, Windows places the translation buffers there; otherwise, they are placed in conventional memory.

When Windows starts in 386 Enhanced mode, it checks to see what free memory is available in the UMB and places the translation buffers there. The problem is that not all of the adapters that use the space give notice that they are there. When both Windows and an adapter attempt to use the space, the system crashes.

Problem:

Your system hangs or crashes in 386 Enhanced mode.

Solution:

You may have a UMB contention problem, which can only occur in 386 Enhanced mode. Try running Windows in Standard mode (**win /s**) to test for a conflict. To determine this for certain, exclude the entire UMB with an EMMEXCLUDE line in the SYSTEM.INI file: Emmexclude = A000-EFFF

You can also use the utility MSD.EXE to display which devices are currently using the UMB address spaces. Some high resolution video boards use the memory area between

C000 and C800. If this is the case, exclude that area using the previous example.

If this solves the problem, you need to determine the position of all your hardware adapters in the UMB. Then you can exclude (with multiple EMMEXCLUDE lines if necessary) only the relevant addresses rather than the entire UMB.

Index

386 enhanced 100, 214
Accessories 2
adding program items 136
application 189, 202
arrange icons 131
associated document 95
associating files 97
auto arrange 133
Borders 10
byte 180
Calculator 3, 28
Calendar 3, 33
Cardfile 3, 52, 53
cascade 131
CD-ROM 182
central processing unit
(CPU) 178, 194
Character map 3, 67
chip 178
clicking 11
client 160
Clipboard 55
Clipboard viewer 5
Clock 3, 24
code 193
color 100, 102
communication programs
192
compatibility 197
compile 193
configuring a printer 119,
120, 121
Control panel 5, 99
control-menu 15

Control-menu box 10
conventional memory 206
copy 50, 51, 75
creating directories 94
creating program groups 134
cut 50, 75
database 191
date 100, 102
delete 50
    program group 139
    program item 139
desktop 10, 100, 105
desktop accessories 23
desktop publishing 192
device fonts 118
digitizers 182
disk 185
disk cache 221
disk drive 185
    floppy 185
    hard 185, 186, 215
DOS 1, 143, 179, 200, 212
DOS applications 143, 144,
    145, 146, 147
    copying from 154
    cutting and pasting 152
DOS prompt 5, 155
double-clicking 11
downloadable fonts 118
drag and drop 126, 127, 138
dragging 11
drivers 100
electronic mail 193
embed 161, 162, 166

editing 165
environments 193
expanded memory 207
extended memory 208
File manager 5, 87
    copy 92
    search 92
fixed space fonts 116
font 116
fonts 100
formatting a disk 94
Games 6
graphical user interface 2
graphics 191
GUI 2
hardware 177, 178
    requirements 195
heaps 211
Help 16, 17
highlighting 48, 49
I-beam 40, 47
icon 10
initialization files 108, 109
input/output devices 180
insertion point 40, 47
installing a printer 119
international 100, 107
keyboard 100, 180
kilobyte 180
language 193
lightpen 182
LIM EMS 208
link 161, 162
loading programs 188
local area network (LAN)
    187, 223
local resource 187
log on 224
Main group 4

maximize 10, 12
Media player 4
megabyte 180
memory 179
menu bar 10
minimize 10, 12
minimize on use 133
modem 185
monitor 183
motherboard 178
mouse 10, 99, 100, 101, 182
moving text 51
multitasking 2
network 227
    connecting drives 228
    installing Windows 224,
    225
    supported 224
    unsupported 224
network card 223
non-Windows application
    copying from 154
non-Windows applications
    144
    copying to 153
Notepad 3, 46
    editing text 47
    entering text 47
object 160
object linking and
embedding (OLE) 159, 160
Object packager 3
opening files 35, 36
operating system 194
options menu 132
outline fonts 117
output devices 182
package 170, 171
Paintbrush 3, 61, 69

drawing basics 72
tools 70, 73
parallel printer ports 120
paste 50
PIF Editor 5
ports 100, 179, 183
parallel 184
serial 184
Print manager 5, 123
printer 100, 183
printer fonts 118
printing 123
program document 95
Program group
closing 15
opening 24
Program groups 6, 130
opening 13
program information files
creating 149
program information files
(PIF) 148
Program Manager 2, 6, 8,
129
proportional fonts 116
pull-down menu 34
quitting a program 27
RAM 179
random access memory
(RAM) 205
raster fonts 117
Recorder 3, 78, 79
restore 10, 12
ROM 179
running under Windows
144
save settings on exit 133
saving a file 41, 42
scanner 182

screen fonts 117
screen savers 106
scroll bars 10, 18
selecting 11
selecting a printer 119
selecting text 48
serial printer ports 120
server 160, 224
setting up a printer 119, 122
setup problems 233
Sizing buttons 10
SMARTDrive 221
software 177, 187
categories 189
sound 100
Sound recorder 4
spreadsheets 190
standard mode 213
StartUp group 6, 140, 143
swap files 216
switching between
programs 58
syntax 193
Sysedit 112
system resources 211
system.ini 111
system.ini file 108
task list 56, 57
templates 188
Terminal 4
tile 130
time 100, 102
toggles 182
touch screen 182
translation buffers 237
troubleshooting 231
TrueType fonts 115, 117
typeface 116
unassociated document 95

undo 50
upper memory block
(UMB) 207
utilities 193
vector fonts 117
voice synthesizers 182
win.ini file 108, 110
window menu commands
    130
Windows 1
    closing 27
    exiting 21
    minimize 27
    moving 25
    opening 7, 8, 95
    parts of 9
    quitting 21
    sizing 25
Windows setup 197
    custom 197
    express 197
    Setup, windows 5
word processing 190
work area 10
workstation 223
Write 3, 61, 62, 63
    fonts 66
    formatting 64
    printing 67
WYSIWYG 115